THE LADY'S CODE

Unlocking the Financial Power of Women

Ester M. Whicker

All Rights Reserved

Table of Contents

INTRODUCTION

The monetary power of ladies has for some time been misjudged, yet entirely no more. **The Lady's Code** opens the monetary capability of ladies all over the place, with a straightforward, yet strong message: Ladies can be strong, fruitful, and monetarily autonomous. No more will ladies be kept down by obsolete thoughts of being a woman. **The Lady's Code** enables ladies to assume command over their funds, to contribute admirably, and to accomplish their monetary objectives.

The Lady's Code is something beyond a book about cash. It is a book about opportunity, about freedom, about self-assurance. A book urges ladies to assume responsibility for their lives, to go with their own choices, to manufacture their own way. A book will have an impact on the manner in which ladies view themselves, and the way the perspectives them.

The Lady's Code is definitely not a convenient solution, a pyramid scheme, or an enchanted arrangement. It is a guide, a manual, a compass for exploring the monetary world. A book will take time, exertion, and devotion to follow, however the prizes will be worth the effort. Ladies who follow the lady's Code will regard themselves as enabled, advanced, and encouraged to accomplish their fantasies.

The Lady's Code is a source of inspiration, a test to ladies wherever to assume command over their lives and their funds. A book requests contemplation, self-reflection, and profound idea. A book will require a lady to inspect her convictions, her propensities, her perspectives, and her ways of behaving. A book will request change, yet the prizes will be perfect. **The Lady's Code** isn't for weak willed, however it is for any individual who is prepared to assume responsibility for her life and her future.

The Lady's Code is something beyond a book about cash. It is a book about freedom, independence, and strengthening. A book provokes ladies to get a sense of ownership with their own lives, to pursue their own choices, and to manufacture their own way. A book will request contemplation, self-assessment, and an eagerness to change. A book will motivate ladies to go after their fantasies and to make the existence they need. A book will change lives.

The Lady's Code isn't a book of sorcery or marvels. It is a book of difficult work, discipline, and devotion. A book will require responsibility and diligence. A book will request tolerance and constancy. A book will move ladies to dig profound, to reach inside themselves, and to track down the solidarity to accomplish their objectives.

The Lady's Code isn't a great fit for everybody. It is for the people who are prepared to invest the energy, who will accomplish the difficult work, and not set in stone to succeed. It is for ladies who are focused on their own development and advancement, who are prepared to assume command over their lives, and who are prepared to assume responsibility for their own monetary future.

The Lady's Code is certainly not a handy solution or an easy route to progress. It is a drawn out arrangement, a way to a superior future, and an arrangement for enduring change. It is an interaction, not an objective. It is an excursion, not an objective. It is a lifestyle, not a prevailing fashion or a pattern. It is a source of inspiration, not a bunch of rules. It is a perspective, not a bunch of convictions.

The Lady's Code isn't a book of sayings or speculations. It is a book of explicit, significant stages, intended to assist ladies with accomplishing their objectives and make the existence they need. A book will enable ladies to assume responsibility for their funds, to make a strong arrangement for their future, and to make their fantasies a reality. A book will have a genuine effect in the existences of ladies.

The Lady's Code isn't simply a book for now. It is a book for the future, for later, and for the future. A book will significantly impact a long time to come. A book will help ladies, everything being equal, in all phases of life, to accomplish their monetary objectives and make the existence they need. A book will motivate and engage ladies to assume command over their lives and to have an effect on the planet. A book will change lives, until the end of time.

The Lady's Code isn't simply a book for ladies. A book for anybody needs to have an effect in their own life, and in the existences of others. A book for anybody needs to make a superior future for them and for people around them. A book for anybody needs to learn, to develop, and to get to the next level.

The Lady's Code is a book about something other than cash. It is a book about values, standards, and needs. It is a book about the main thing throughout everyday life. A book will provoke you to ponder what you truly need, and how you will accomplish it. A book will make you question your suppositions and your convictions. A book will make you think, and a book will make you develop.

The Lady's Code is a book that will challenge you, yet it will likewise uphold you. It will push you to turn into your best self, yet it will likewise furnish you with the instruments and assets you really want to arrive.

A book will assist you with building a strong starting point for your life, and to make a future that is based on that establishment. A book will give you the certainty to confront any test and to conquer any snag.

The Lady's Code is a book that will move you to make a move, yet likewise a book will give you the mental fortitude to make that move. A book will give you the solidarity to push through your feelings of dread and to push ahead. A book will show you the worth of tirelessness, of constancy, and of strength. A book will show you the force of assurance, and of never surrendering. A book will make serious areas of strength for you.

The Lady's Code is a book that will make you contemplate the central issues throughout everyday life. A book will make you question what you accept and why you trust it. A book will move you to think fundamentally, to be interested, and to learn.

A book will make you question all that you assume you know, and all that you underestimate. A book will make you question the actual idea of the real world.

The Lady's Code is a book that will make you question the significance of life, the idea of presence, and the reason for humankind. A book will cause you to think about your position in the universe, and your part at the end of the day. A book will make you question your convictions about the world, and about yourself. A book will compel you to defy your most profound feelings of trepidation, and to confront your most prominent difficulties.

The monetary power of ladies is frequently ignored and underestimated, however it is an awe-inspiring phenomenon. Ladies are taking extraordinary steps in the realm of money, and are transforming the universe of business and financial planning.

They are presently not content to be latent beneficiaries of monetary data; they are assuming command over their own monetary fates and making informed choices about their cash. They are assuming responsibility for their own monetary fates, and are reclassifying being a monetarily effective lady.

There are many justifications for why the monetary force of ladies is so significant. For one's purposes, ladies control a lot of the world's riches. They are a developing power in the labor force, and are getting increasingly more cash consistently. They are additionally turning out to be increasingly taught, and are finding out increasingly more about cash and money.

They are assuming command over their own funds, and are turning out to be progressively persuasive in the monetary world. They are rocking the boat and separating hindrances, and are reshaping the manner in which we contemplate cash and financial planning.

Moreover, the monetary influence of ladies is significant in light of the fact that it is assisting with shutting the orientation abundance hole. Ladies have customarily been in a difficult spot with regards to procuring and collecting riches, however they are currently taking extraordinary steps around here.

They are bringing in more cash, putting away more cash, and making their voices heard in the monetary world. They are requesting balance and regard, and are clarifying that they won't make with anything less. They are reclassifying being a lady, and are demonstrating the way that ladies can be similarly basically as fruitful as men with regards to cash and fund.

At long last, the monetary force of ladies is significant in light of the fact that it is assisting with making an all the more and impartial society. At the point when ladies have more monetary power, they can utilize that ability to battle for civil rights and correspondence.

They can make change in their networks and on the planet, and can utilize their monetary ability to have a genuine effect. They are utilizing their cash to help causes they care about, and to make the world a superior spot for everybody. They are making a tradition of strengthening, and are motivating others to do likewise.

Notwithstanding these advantages, the monetary force of ladies is likewise emphatically affecting the economy. Ladies are turning out to be progressively significant purchasers, and are driving monetary development in numerous nations. They are beginning organizations, making position, and adding to the general strength of the economy.

They are significantly having an impact on the manner in which organizations work, and are transforming the universe of money and financial matters. They are demonstrating the way that ladies can find success in any field, and that they ought to be considered carefully or excused.

There are numerous manners by which the monetary force of ladies is emphatically affecting the world. For instance, ladies are progressively taking on positions of authority in the monetary business. They are turning out to be more associated with navigation, and are impacting the heading of the business.

They are additionally utilizing their monetary ability to help causes that are mean a lot to them, like ecological manageability and civil rights. Furthermore, they are altering how cash is utilized and made due, by advancing monetary education and mindful spending.

Chapter One

Money is a Woman's Closest companion

Money is many times considered a no theme, particularly for ladies. Notwithstanding, cash can be one of the best devices to engage ladies and give them enough opportunity and autonomy. The initial step to making monetary progress is to perceive that cash isn't something to be dreaded or stayed away from, but instead something to be embraced.

Cash can be a wellspring of strengthening and security and with the right information and instruments, ladies can assume command over their funds and make the existence they need.

In this section, we will investigate the various ways that cash can be a lady's dearest companion.
One way cash can be a lady's dearest companion is through the power of self multiplying dividends.

By beginning to contribute early and consistently, ladies can exploit the sorcery of accumulated dividends and watch their cash develop dramatically over the long haul. For instance, on the off chance that a lady contributes $100 each month at a 7% pace of return for a considerable length of time, she will have more than $158,000 toward the finish of that time span. That is over two times her underlying venture! By understanding the influence of accumulating funds, ladies can assume command over their monetary future and bring in their cash work for them.

Another way that cash can be a lady's closest companion is through planning. By making and adhering to a spending plan, ladies can bring in certainty that their cash is being spent shrewdly and lined up with their qualities and objectives. There are a wide range of planning techniques, like the envelope framework, the 50/30/20 rule, and zero-based planning.
Regardless of which strategy is utilised, the key is to track down a framework that works for every person and stick to it.

Planning can likewise assist ladies with recognizing and taking out superfluous costs, opening up cash to be utilised for additional significant things.

As well as planning, one more significant monetary device for ladies is objective setting. Defining monetary objectives can assist with providing guidance and inspiration to save and contribute. By separating huge objectives into more modest, more reasonable advances, ladies can cause their objectives to feel not so much overpowering but rather more reachable.

For instance, on the off chance that a lady will likely purchase a house, she can separate that objective into more modest objectives, for example, putting something aside for an initial instalment, further developing her FICO rating, and exploring contract choices.
With every little objective achieved, she can feel more certain and in charge of her monetary future.

Another way that cash can be a woman's closest companion is through arranging.

Ladies are frequently told to be calm and pleasant, however with regards to individual budget; this can set them back a huge load of cash.

Studies have shown that ladies who arrange their compensations and other monetary issues can acquire a huge number of dollars more throughout the span of their lifetime. By figuring out how to haggle successfully, ladies can get a greater amount of what they merit and gain a feeling of certainty and strengthening. Furthermore, they can act as good examples for different ladies and help to close the orientation pay hole.

Another significant way that cash can be a woman's closest companion is through safeguarding her resources. This incorporates doing whatever it takes to safeguard against monetary extortion, like areas of strength for utilising and being careful about phishing tricks.

It additionally remembers having the right insurance

contracts for place, like health care coverage, disaster protection, and property protection. By avoiding potential risk, ladies can defend their funds and find harmony in their psyche. Making a monetary arrangement in the event of a crisis, for example, an employment misfortune or clinical crisis is likewise significant.

To wrap things up, perhaps the main way that cash can be a woman's closest companion is through putting resources into her self-improvement.

This can incorporate things like taking classes, going to studios, and perusing books on individual accounting and effective financial planning.

It can likewise remember effective money management for one's well being and prosperity, like eating quality food, working out, and getting sufficient rest.

By putting resources into one, ladies can work on their

lives and their funds over the long haul. All things considered, the most significant resource anybody can have is their own wellbeing and prosperity.

While cash can be an incredible asset for ladies, it is critical to recollect that not by any means the only thing matters. Ladies ought to likewise focus on their connections, interests, and reason throughout everyday life. By finding harmony among cash and other significant things, ladies can make a satisfying and balanced life.

Eventually, satisfaction isn't estimated by the size of one's ledger, yet by the nature of one's connections, wellbeing, and generally feeling of prosperity.

It is likewise important that monetary autonomy appears to be unique for everybody.

For certain ladies, it might mean having the option to bear the cost of a specific way of life or way of life. For other people, it might mean having the option to resign early or seek after their fantasy vocation.

The key is to characterise what monetary autonomy resembles for every person and afterward do whatever it takes to accomplish it. There is no one size-fits-all arrangement and every lady should track down her own way to independence from the rat race.

It is likewise worth focusing on that monetary freedom isn't an objective, however an excursion. Life is loaded with highs and lows, and monetary conditions can change over the long haul.

What makes the biggest difference is gaining predictable headway and remaining strong notwithstanding challenges.

Regardless of whether there are mishaps, it is critical to recollect that progress isn't straight 100% of the time.

Each step in the right direction is a triumph, regardless of how little it might appear.

While there are numerous monetary points to examine, recollecting the profound side of money is likewise significant. Numerous ladies have a confounded relationship with cash, and it is frequently attached to previous encounters and youth messages about cash.

It is vital to recognize and manage any cash blocks or gloomy sentiments around cash to make a solid relationship with it. This might include analysing one's qualities, convictions, and feelings around cash, and making moves to rethink any pessimistic convictions.

Notwithstanding the profound side of cash, one more significant part of monetary wellbeing is monetary education. This incorporates information about planning, effective money management, charges, and other monetary ideas. While monetary proficiency is frequently connected with maths abilities, it is more about figuring out the monetary framework and having the option to pursue informed choices.

It is assessed that only 33% of grown-ups in the US are monetarily educated. This implies that many individuals are not furnished with the information they need to settle on the best monetary choices for their lives.

One method for further developing monetary proficiency is through instruction. This should be possible in schools, work environments, and local area associations. Monetary proficiency instruction ought to be available to individuals of any age and foundations. It ought to likewise be pertinent to the particular necessities and difficulties of individuals getting the instruction.

For instance, monetary proficiency instruction for youthful grown-ups ought to zero in on subjects, for example, planning and putting something aside for the future, while monetary proficiency training for more established grown-ups may zero in addition on retirement arranging and domain arranging.

Cash can be a Woman's closest companion with regards to expanding her conviction that all is good, control, and opportunity.

Cash can enable ladies to decide, face challenges, and put resources into themselves and their prospects. With cash, ladies can have the assets to work on their personal satisfaction and seek after their interests.

Cash can likewise permit ladies to have more options and open doors in their connections, profession, and by and large prosperity. To put it plainly, cash can be a companion that engages ladies to carry on with their best lives.

Cash can likewise be a Woman's dearest companion with regards to building monetary freedom. Monetary autonomy implies being able to meet one's fundamental requirements without depending on others. This can be a strong inclination for ladies, who have generally been monetarily reliant upon others, like their spouses or fathers.

By expanding their monetary proficiency and assuming command over their funds, ladies can acquire a feeling of organisation and freedom that can work on their lives.

Notwithstanding security, control, and autonomy, cash can likewise carry genuine serenity to ladies. At the point when ladies have a solid sense of safety, they can zero in on different parts of their lives, like family, companions, and interests.

Monetary security can lessen pressure and nervousness, prompting work on physical and psychological wellness. It can likewise prompt additional satisfying connections and a more noteworthy feeling of prosperity. By giving true serenity, cash can permit ladies to make every moment count.

While cash can be a Woman's closest companion, it is critical to recall that not by any means the only thing matters. Cash is just an instrument that can be utilised to accomplish one's objectives and values. Without a reasonable feeling of what is vital to them, ladies can wind up pursuing cash with no genuine feeling of direction or satisfaction.

For instance, a few ladies might forfeit time with their families or companions to seek after more cash. Others might secure themselves working in positions that they hate, however that compensate fairly. Eventually, cash ought to be utilised to support the things that mean quite a bit to every person.

As well as having an unmistakable feeling of direction, having a sound connection with money is likewise significant. Certain individuals might become fixated on cash, zeroing in on riches and material belongings to the detriment of their prosperity.

This can prompt a pattern of overspending, obligation, and even dependence. Then again, certain individuals might feel regretful about burning through cash or dread becoming materialistic. In any case, cash needn't bother with being viewed as a wellspring of one or the other fixation or culpability. Rather, it tends to be seen as a device to be utilised capably and carefully, to support a satisfying life.

At last, it is critical to recollect that cash isn't the best way to quantify achievement. There are numerous alternate ways of tracking down satisfaction and joy, like connections, learning, innovative pursuits, and helping other people. While cash can give security and a feeling of control, it isn't the main proportion of a fruitful life. With regards to ladies and cash, a reasonable and insightful methodology is the way to genuine joy and satisfaction.

Cash can satisfy a Woman's life in various ways. As a matter of some importance, it can give security and steadiness. At the point when a lady has sufficient cash to cover her essential requirements, she can feel a feeling of safety and harmony. This security can permit her to zero in on different parts of her life, like her connections and interests.

Moreover, cash can furnish a lady with the opportunity to seek after her objectives and dreams.

It can give her the adaptability to face challenges and depend on her instinct, without stressing over monetary imperatives.

Cash can likewise be utilised to fabricate and reinforce connections. For instance, it can permit a lady to invest quality energy with her friends and family, by taking them on excursions or getting those encounters and gifts. It can likewise give the assets to assist relatives in the midst of hardship.

At last, cash can be utilised to have an effect on the planet. A lady with cash can uphold causes she thinks often about, whether through magnanimous gifts or chipping in her time. By involving her cash along these lines, she can feel a feeling of satisfaction and association.

On a more profound level, cash can likewise be a wellspring of self-awareness. It can give a lady the assets to seek after training and self-awareness, which can prompt more noteworthy mindfulness and satisfaction.

Cash can likewise be utilised to investigate otherworldliness, for example, through withdrawals, reflection classes, and profound advising. So, cash can be utilised in manners that go past material belongings and monetary security. It tends to be an instrument for change, development, and association.

While cash can be utilised in numerous positive ways, it's memorable critical that not by any means the only thing gives joy. Many investigations have shown that past a specific degree of pay, extra cash doesn't fundamentally increment satisfaction.

There are different elements that are more significant for satisfaction, like significant connections, a feeling of direction, and feeling associated with an option that could be greater than one. A day to day existence loaded up with these things can profoundly satisfy, regardless of cash.

Notwithstanding connections and reason, there are numerous different variables that add to bliss. For instance, great actual wellbeing, an uplifting perspective on life, and solid socially encouraging groups of people can all increase satisfaction.

Research has likewise shown that having appreciation and relishing life's straightforward delights can give pleasure. At long last, captivating in exercises that bring flow, or a feeling of being totally caught up in the thing you're doing, can prompt sensations of bliss and satisfaction. Cash may not be the way to satisfaction, but rather these elements are many times considerably more significant over the long haul.

Monetary freedom for a lady implies having command over her own monetary fate, as opposed to depending on others for monetary help. This incorporates having sufficient cash to cover her fundamental necessities, as well as the capacity to save and contribute for what's in store.

Monetary freedom additionally implies having the information and abilities to deal with her own funds, and the certainty to make choices about her cash. It isn't really about having a specific measure of cash, yet rather about being in charge of one's own monetary life.

One vital calculation accomplishing monetary freedom is having a strong arrangement set up. This could incorporate laying out monetary objectives, making a spending plan, and putting something aside for what's in store. It is likewise essential to construct a backup stash, so startling costs don't crash a lady's monetary objectives.

Contributing admirably is one more significant piece of the arrangement, as it can assist with developing one's cash over the long run. At last, it is essential to audit and change the arrangement as life conditions change. Accomplishing monetary freedom calls for investment, persistence, and an eagerness to learn and adjust.

One more vital part of monetary autonomy is developing sound monetary propensities. This incorporates abstaining from overspending, and opposing motivation buys. Fostering the discipline to save and contribute routinely is likewise significant.

It is additionally vital to be aware of one's spending and monetary decisions, and to address whether they line up with one's qualities and objectives. Furthermore, it is useful to monitor one's monetary advancement and celebrate triumphs en route.

These propensities may not be not difficult to grow, however they are fundamental for accomplishing monetary autonomy.

This expression has a few translations; however one normal comprehension is that having cash can furnish ladies with a feeling of safety and opportunity. Cash can assist with covering essential necessities, like food, haven, and attire. It can likewise permit ladies to seek after objectives, like voyaging or beginning a business.

Moreover, having cash can give ladies the adaptability to go with choices in view of their qualities, as opposed to absolutely on monetary need. While cash may not be truly significant throughout everyday life, it tends to be an important device for ladies to carry on with an existence of direction and satisfaction.

Significance

1. Cash gives ladies monetary security and inner serenity.

2. Cash permits ladies to put something aside for the future and plan for surprising occasions.

3. Cash can be utilised to help causes that ladies care about, for example, good causes or civil rights issues.

4. Cash offers ladies the chance to put resources into their own schooling, abilities, and future vocation.

5. Cash permits ladies to seek after leisure activities and interests that give them pleasure.

6. Cash empowers ladies to purchase presents for loved ones.

7. Cash permits ladies to travel and investigate new spots.

8. Cash can be utilised to give ladies monetary autonomy and independence from dependence on others.

9. Cash gives ladies more command over their lives and a

feeling of organisation.

10. Cash permits ladies to pursue decisions in view of what is really essential to them, as opposed to just what is monetarily pragmatic.

11. Cash can be a wellspring of strengthening, particularly for ladies who have generally been denied admittance to monetary assets.

12. Cash permits ladies to make monetary strength for them as well as their families.

13. Cash offers ladies the chance to make generational abundance for their youngsters and grandkids.
14. Cash assists ladies with building an inheritance and makes a positive effect on their general surroundings.

15. Cash can be utilised to help make that matter, like ladies' wellbeing, instruction, and security.

16. Cash permits ladies to give to noble causes or causes that mean a lot to them.

17. Cash offers ladies the chance to support grants or awards for different ladies.

18. Cash empowers ladies to begin their own organisations and set out open doors for different ladies.

19. Cash furnishes ladies with the resources to buy quality items and administrations that work on their lives.

20. Cash permits ladies to get to quality medical care and other significant administrations that they could not in any case have the option to bear.

21. Cash furnishes ladies with the capacity to carry on with an existence of value and solace.

22. Cash offers ladies the chance to create financial stability and become monetarily autonomous.

23. Cash permits ladies to invest more energy with their families and companions.

24. Cash can be utilised to make a more agreeable and pleasant way of life.

25. Cash gives ladies the capacity to have a constructive outcome on their networks.

26. Cash is a device that can be utilised to assist ladies with accomplishing their objectives and dreams.

27. Cash gives ladies the opportunity to face challenges and seek after new open doors.

28. Cash furnishes ladies with the adaptability to adjust to evolving conditions.

29. Cash is a type of taking care of oneself and confidence, as dealing with one's essential requirements and prosperity can be utilised.

30. Cash permits ladies to partake; it could be said of safety and soundness in their lives.

31. Cash is a significant device that can be utilised to make an existence of direction, importance, and satisfaction.

32. Cash engages ladies to be their best selves.

33. Cash can be utilised to advance orientation fairness by shutting the orientation pay hole and giving admittance to assets and amazing open doors for ladies.

34. Cash can be utilised to battle orientation generalisations and inclinations.

35. Cash gives ladies the capacity to help causes that advance orientation fairness and civil rights.

36. Cash empowers ladies to be good examples for people in the future of ladies.

37. Cash assists with separating boundaries that keep ladies from accomplishing their maximum capacity.

38. Cash empowers ladies to get to quality schooling and prepare open doors.

39. Cash gives ladies the capacity to seek after their interests and interests.

40. Cash enables ladies to seek after advanced education and further their professions.

41. Cash permits ladies to carry on with a unique kind of energy picking.

42. Cash is a device that can be utilised to have an effect on the planet.

43. Cash enables ladies to make some noise and promoters for them and others.

44. Cash permits ladies to partake in the worldwide economy.

45. Cash furnishes ladies with a stage to share their accounts and encounters.

46. Cash is an instrument that can be utilised to make a fairer and only world for all individuals.

47. Cash offers ladies the chance to rock the boat and separate orientation obstructions.

48. Cash is an instrument that can be utilised to advance social and financial versatility for ladies.

49. Cash is an asset that can be utilised to assist ladies with accessing medical services, schooling, and other fundamental requirements.

50. Cash gives ladies a feeling of organisation and command over their own lives.

At last, cash is a strong asset that can be utilised to enable ladies and make positive change on the planet.

Chapter Two

Know Your Numbers

Know your numbers is the second part of **"The Lady's**

Code," and it centres on the significance of figuring out one's monetary circumstance. In this section, we will investigate the various numbers that ladies ought to know about, like their pay, costs, reserve funds, obligation, and total assets. We will likewise take a gander at how to follow these numbers and use them to make a spending plan and put forth monetary objectives. At long last, we will examine the significance of monitoring one's FICO rating and how to further develop it.

Realising one's numbers is an urgent initial phase in making monetary progress. To start, having an unmistakable comprehension of one's income is significant.

This incorporates knowing how much cash one acquires every month and the wellsprings of that pay. It is likewise vital to follow any extra types of revenue, for example, rewards, commissions, or second jobs.

When a lady knows her pay, she can start to make a

financial plan and decide how much cash she has accessible to spend every month. Moreover, understanding one's expenses is significant. This incorporates following every single customary cost, like lease, utilities, food, transportation, and other fixed costs.

Notwithstanding standard costs, it is likewise critical to track and spend plans for sporadic costs, for example, vehicle fixes, hospital expenses, and home upkeep. Saving cash for surprising costs, for example, an employment misfortune or an emergency is likewise significant.

When a lady knows her normal and unpredictable costs, she can make a spending plan and put forth monetary objectives. This spending plan ought to incorporate setting aside cash for crises, as well with respect to longer-term objectives, like purchasing a home or resigning.

By understanding her pay and costs, a lady can start to settle on informed conclusions about her funds and assume command over her monetary future.

As well as knowing pay and costs, it is additionally critical to know about one's investment funds and obligations. How much cash one has in reserve funds can give a pad to crises or surprising costs.

A lady ought to likewise know about any obligation she has, including the sum owed, the financing cost, and the reimbursement terms.

Realising this data can assist her with making an arrangement to take care of obligations and further develop her FICO rating. It is likewise critical to comprehend the various sorts of obligation, for example, exorbitant interest MasterCard obligation and low-interest understudy loans.

One last number that is critical to know is one's total assets. This is the complete worth of one's resources, like reserve funds, ventures, and property, short of any obligations. Realising one's total assets can be a useful method for following monetary headway and settling on informed conclusions around one's funds.

For instance, a lady with positive total assets might have the option to make the most of chances, like putting resources into the financial exchange or beginning a business. A lady with negative total assets might have to zero in on paying off her obligation prior to taking other monetary actions.

Understanding these numbers is just the most important phase in making a monetarily solid life. The subsequent stage is to put forth objectives and make an arrangement to accomplish them. This could incorporate laying out an objective to save a specific measure of cash every month or to take care of a specific measure of obligation every year.

Having explicit, quantifiable objectives can assist a lady with keeping focused and gaining ground towards monetary achievement. It is additionally essential to follow headway and make changes in accordance with the arrangement on a case by case basis.
The key is to be patient and to celebrate triumphs en route. Monetary achievement is certainly not a short-term process, yet rather a drawn out venture.

As well as defining monetary objectives, making a spending plan and sticking to it is likewise significant.

A spending plan is an arrangement for how to burn through cash every month, and it ought to consider both pay and costs.

Making a financial plan can assist a lady with focusing on

her spending and ensure that she is living inside her means. There is a wide range of techniques for making a financial plan, like the 50/30/20 strategy or the envelope technique. The key is to track down a strategy that works for the individual and to be adaptable as conditions change.

One more significant part of monetary wellbeing is figuring out how to deal with feelings around cash. This can be a difficult undertaking, as cash is frequently connected with sensations of stress, uneasiness, and responsibility. Nonetheless, it is vital to recollect that cash is only a device, and that it ought not to be the wellspring of pessimistic feelings.

All things considered, attempt to zero in on the positive parts of cash, for example, the capacity to accomplish objectives and make a seriously satisfying life. In the event that pessimistic feelings continue, it could be useful to search out a monetary specialist or a care group to figure out these problems.

At last, one of the main parts of monetary wellbeing is making positive cash outlook. This includes moving one's reasoning from a position of shortage to a position of overflow. It is likewise about recognizing and praising one's victories, instead of zeroing in on previous slip-ups.

At the point when a lady has a positive cash mentality, she is bound to settle on great monetary choices and to remain spurred on her excursion to monetary health. Far to develop positive cash outlook incorporates rehearsing appreciation, picturing achievement, and staying away from correlations with others.

Finding an opportunity to teach oneself about cash is one more significant part of monetary wellbeing. There is an abundance of data accessible on individual budgets, from books and web recordings to online assets and classes.

Finding out about subjects, for example, planning,

effective money management, and saving can be enabling and can prompt better monetary choices. It is likewise vital to keep awake to date on monetary news and patterns, so one can make informed choices about cash. This should be possible by perusing monetary news locales, paying attention to webcasts, or buying into bulletins.

One incredible asset for finding out about individual budgets is the site and application Mint. Mint is a free instrument that permits clients to follow their spending, make financial plans, and put forth objectives.

The site likewise has articles and guides on different monetary points, from financial planning to purchase a home.

Another helpful asset is the blog The Straightforward Dollar, which offers viable and straightforward counsel on individual accounting. What's more, for the individuals who like to learn through digital broadcasts, the NPR show Commercial centre Cash is an incredible asset for staying aware of the most recent monetary news.

Notwithstanding on the web assets, there are likewise many books accessible on the subject of individual budget. Get them and peruse. These books give viable exhortations on points like saving, effective financial planning, and taking care of obligations. They likewise offer experiences into the mental parts of individual budgets, for example, how to change one's relationship with cash.

For the people who are keen on a more top to bottom comprehension of individual budgets, there are likewise certificate programs accessible. The Affirmed Monetary Organizer (CFP) assignment is the most notable monetary confirmation. To procure this certificate, people should finish coursework and breeze through a thorough test.

There are likewise projects like the Licensed Monetary Guide (AFC) certificate, which is explicitly intended for people who need to help other people with their funds. What's more, for the individuals who need to find out about effective money management, the Contracted Monetary Examiner (CFA) assignment is an exceptionally regarded certificate.

As well as understanding books and procuring certificates, there are likewise various sites and applications that can assist with explicit parts of individual accounting. For instance, Mint is a famous site and application that assists with planning, charge following, and money management.

The Individual Capital application is one more helpful

device for following funds, and it likewise offers customised monetary guidance. Furthermore, for the people who are keen on setting aside cash, the Honey expansion for Chrome and Firefox is an incredible method for tracking down coupons and limits on internet shopping.

While there are numerous assets accessible for finding out about individual budgets, it is likewise essential to find the strategy that turns out best for every person.

Certain individuals like to understand books, while others might like to watch recordings or pay attention to digital broadcasts.

There is nobody the right method for finding out about individual budgets, so it means a lot to try different things with various strategies and find what works best. It is likewise vital to recall that finding out about individual budgets is a long lasting cycle, and it is never past time to begin.

While laying out monetary objectives, contemplating both the present moment and long haul is significant. Transient objectives might incorporate things like putting something aside for a get-away or taking care of a charge card balance.

Long haul objectives might incorporate things like putting something aside for retirement or taking care of a home loan.

It is likewise vital to think about how individual conditions, for example, having kids or evolving positions, may affect monetary objectives. While defining objectives, it is likewise critical to consider what kind of way of life is wanted and how much cash will be expected to help that way of life.

One significant thought while pondering a way of life is

the possibility of "independence from the rat race." Independence from the rat race implies having sufficient cash saved and contributed so that work becomes discretionary. This might be accomplished through a blend of living underneath one's method, saving and money management, and tracking down ways of producing recurring, automated revenue.

Eventually, independence from the rat race can give individuals the adaptability to settle on decisions that line up with their qualities and objectives.

One more significant part of monetary arranging is planning for unforeseen occasions. Nobody can foresee the future, yet it is essential to have an arrangement set up in the event of crises, like employment misfortune, sickness, or cataclysmic events.

Far to get ready for the startling incorporate having a backup stash, having sufficient protection inclusion, and making an arrangement for managing obligation. It is additionally vital to remain informed about monetary news and changes in the economy, with the goal that one can be ready for any likely monetary difficulties.

As you pursue accomplishing your monetary objectives, focusing on your own bliss and prosperity is additionally significant. While cash can be utilised to purchase material merchandise and encounters, it is critical to recall that it can't buy joy.

Research has shown that once fundamental necessities are met, cash doesn't essentially affect bliss.
All things considered, things like connections, significant work, and a feeling of direction bigly affect general satisfaction. Thus, while it is essential to have monetary objectives, it means quite a bit to track down ways of getting a charge out of life right now.

For women, monetary education can assist with making everything fair and give a feeling of strengthening.

Overall, ladies acquire not as much as men and are bound to remove time from the labour force to really focus on youngsters or older family members. This can prompt lower lifetime profit and less monetary security.

In any case, by finding out about individual accounting, ladies can make informed choices about their cash and make an arrangement for their future. This can assist them with being in charge of their own lives and pursue decisions that line up with their qualities and objectives.

Monetary education is likewise significant for ladies since it can assist with shutting the orientation abundance hole. Overall, ladies are less abundant than men, and this hole develops with age. The orientation abundance hole is brought about by various elements, including the compensation hole, the abundance hole, and different monetary needs and ways of behaving.

By turning out to be monetarily proficient, ladies can figure out how to do whatever it takes to close this hole, like saving and contributing more, requesting raises and advancements, and anticipating retirement.

Another way that monetary education can help ladies is by assisting them with keeping away from monetary maltreatment.

Monetary maltreatment is a type of aggressive behaviour at home that affects controlling and limiting an individual's admittance to monetary assets. This can be a huge hindrance to leaving a harmful relationship, and it can likewise have long haul ramifications for an individual's monetary security.

By finding out about individual budgets, ladies can figure

out how to perceive the indications of monetary maltreatment and do whatever it may take to safeguard them. They can likewise figure out how to fabricate their own monetary autonomy so they are not subject to an oppressive accomplice.

At long last, monetary education can assist ladies with building local areas and backing one another. At the point when ladies are monetarily proficient, they can impart data and assets to different ladies, and help to fabricate an organisation of help.

This can be particularly useful for ladies who might not approach customary monetary assets, like family or companions.

By making a local area of monetarily educated ladies, we can assist with shutting the orientation abundance hole and make a fairer world for everybody. How have you utilised your monetary education to help different ladies?

Ways Women Can Know Their Numbers

The following are different ways that women can know their numbers:

- Track your month to month spending.

- Screen your FICO rating.

- Make a spending plan.

- Know your total assets.

- Ascertain your relationship of outstanding debt to take home pay.

- Screen your retirement reserve funds.

- Realise your Federal retirement aide benefits.

- Know your protection and inclusion.

- Grasp your assessment obligation.

- Realise your home arrangement.

- Grasp your speculations.

- Track your total assets over the long run.

- Screen your credit report.

- Monitor your ways of managing money.

Here are an additional ways of knowing your numbers:

- Get coordinated and monitor the entirety of your monetary data.

- Utilise individual accounting programming or applications to help you track and deal with your funds.

- Employ a monetary counsel to assist you with making an arrangement and keep tabs on your development.

- Understand books, online journals, and different assets to become familiar with individual budgets.

- Join a local area of ladies who are keen on individual budgets.

- Take a class on an individual budget.

- Search for a tutor who can assist you with your funds.

On the off chance that you're searching for much more ways of knowing your numbers, attempt these ideas:

- Audit your credit report consistently.

- Survey your bank and speculation explanations

consistently.

- Gauge your retirement needs.

- Gauge your medical services costs in retirement.

- Take a gander at the financing costs on your credits and obligations.

- Ensure you're on target to take care of your obligation.

- Watch out for expansion and what it means for your funds.

- Stay aware of recent developments and what they mean for the economy.

- Realise the financing costs on your investment accounts.

Familiar Ways Women Can Know Their Numbers

Here are another, more uncommon ways of knowing your numbers:

- Sort out your lifetime income potential.

- Gauge your future.

- Comprehend the amount you'll have to cover your burial service and end-of-life costs.

- Comprehend the worth of your home and some other resources you own.

- Think about the expense of long haul care.

- Comprehend the worth of your Government managed retirement benefits.

- Figure out the worth of your annuity and different advantages.

- Decide the expense of your side interests and different exercises.

- Think about the expense of schooling for yourself or your relatives.

One more method for realising your numbers is to contemplate your objectives and what they mean for your funds. Here are a few models:

- What is it that you need to accomplish in the following five years?

- What are your drawn out objectives for your profession?

- What are your objectives for your loved ones?

- What are your objectives for your wellbeing and health?

- What are your objectives for rewarding your local area?

- What are your objectives for your otherworldly life?

- What are your objectives for your self-awareness?
- What are your objectives for your leisure activities and interests?

At last, here are a particular ways of realising your numbers connected with your costs:

- Make a rundown of your proper costs, like lodging, food, transportation, and utilities.

- Make a rundown of your variable costs, like diversion, dress, and eating out.

- Make a rundown of your optional costs, like travel,

gifts, and side interests.

- Gauge the expense of childcare, instruction, and other ward costs.

- Comprehend the expenses related with your clinical and dental consideration.

- Comprehend the expenses related to your pets.

- Think about the expenses of your home upkeep and repairs.

When you have a decent comprehension of your costs, you can begin to search for ways of lessening your spending. A few thoughts include:

- Arranging your bills, like utilities, links, and the web.

- Lessening your food costs by cooking at home and utilising coupons.

- Decreasing your transportation costs via carpooling, taking public travel, or trekking.

- Lessening your apparel costs by shopping at secondhand shops or transfer shops.

Chapter Three

Make Your Money Work for You

Make Your Money Work for You is the title of the third part of "**The Lady's Code**."

In this part, we'll probably investigate the main parts of Making your cash work for you, including money management, saving, and making a monetary arrangement. We'll likewise take a gander at ways of safeguarding your monetary prosperity and ways of bringing in your cash work for you in the long haul.

Monetary arranging is fundamental for all ladies, regardless of what their pay level or phase of life. With a strong monetary arrangement, you can assume command over your cash and make it work for you, rather than the opposite way around.

The most important phase in bringing in your cash work for you is to figure out your monetary objectives. Would you like to have the option to serenely resign? Would you like to accommodate your loved ones? Would you like to take care of your obligations? When you understand what you need to accomplish, you can begin to make an arrangement to get it going.

Your monetary arrangement ought to incorporate a financial plan, a reserve funds plan, and a venture methodology. It's likewise critical to have a backup stash, to ensure you're ready for startling costs.

Your financial plan is the groundwork of your monetary arrangement. It's a guide for how you will spend your cash, and it's fundamental for ensuring you're on target to accomplish your objectives. Your spending plan ought to incorporate the entirety of your pay and costs, so you know precisely where your cash is going.

It ought to likewise incorporate some space for error for startling costs, so you don't need to stress over going over your spending plan.

When you have a financial plan set up, you can begin to zero in on your reserve funds plan. Setting aside cash is fundamental for building your monetary security, and there are different ways of getting it done.

One of the main pieces of your investment funds plan is

your just-in-case account. This is a reserve of cash that you can use if there should be an occurrence of a crisis, like an employment misfortune, a doctor's visit expense, or a home fix. Preferably, your secret stash ought to be sufficient to cover your costs for somewhere around three to a half year. Along these lines, you'll make them inhale room if something unforeseen occurs.

Notwithstanding your secret stash, you ought to likewise think about putting something aside for retirement.
The prior you begin putting something aside for retirement, the additional time your cash needs to develop. Beginning contemplating your future monetary security is rarely too soon.

When you have your financial plan and reserve funds plan set up, you can begin to contemplate effective money management. Contributing is an incredible method for developing your cash after some time, and there are different choices accessible to you. You can put resources into stocks, securities, shared assets, from there, the sky's the limit. It means a lot to converse with a monetary guide to ensure you're picking the right ventures for your objectives.

Keep in mind; it's never too soon or beyond any good time to begin effective financial planning. Regardless of whether you're not ready to put away a truckload of cash, beginning somewhere is significant. Each and every piece counts!

As well as saving and effective money management, it's likewise vital to safeguard your monetary prosperity. This remembers things like having the right insurance contracts for place and making an arrangement in the event that you become sick or debilitated. It's likewise really smart to have a home arrangement set up, so your friends and family understand what to do on the off chance that something happens to you.

Ultimately, remember to zero in on your monetary training. The more familiar you are with cash, the better prepared you'll be to settle on savvy monetary choices. There are a lot of assets accessible to assist you with finding out more, including books, sites, and classes.

Something last to remember is that your monetary arrangement ought to be adaptable. Your life will change over the long haul, and your monetary arrangement ought to have the option to adjust to those changes. For instance, assuming that you get hitched or have kids, your spending plan and reserve funds plan will probably should be changed.

The equivalent is valid in the event that you experience an employment cutback or an adjustment of pay. Being adaptable and open to change is critical to keeping a sound monetary life.

It's likewise vital to recollect that cash isn't all that matters. While it's vital to be monetarily mindful, it's additionally essential to appreciate life and not let cash consume all your contemplations.

Eventually, the main thing is to track down an equilibrium that works for you. Make it a point to change your arrangement as your life altering events, and remember to partake in the excursion. Cash is an instrument that can be utilised to make a superior life, yet not by any means the only thing that matters. The main thing is to track down bliss and satisfaction in your life.

In this way, to summarise, **"The Lady's Code"** is tied in with assuming command over your monetary life and making that employer you. This plan ought to be adaptable, and it ought to zero in on your extraordinary objectives and conditions.

One last suggestion is to find a responsibility accomplice. This can be a companion, relative, or monetary counsellor who can assist you with keeping focused and urge you to arrive at your objectives. Having somebody to converse with about your funds can be a tremendous assistance, and it can make the interaction much less overwhelming.

These lines, that's it! These are the central issues of "The Woman's Code." Keep in mind; you don't need to be a specialist to assume command over your monetary life. Simply start with a couple of little advances, and you'll be shocked at how far you can go.

I'm happy you're so keen on diving deeper into individual accounting! One method for keeping on learning is to look at a portion of the incredible assets that are accessible on the web. The Monetary Proficiency and Schooling Commission site has heaps of supportive data, and there are additionally numerous incredible online journals and webcasts out there. The more you know, the better prepared you'll be to make shrewd choices about your cash.

I'm generally glad to visit about cash, so go ahead and return any time. I'm continuously learning and growing my insight, so I'm certain we'll have a lot to discuss from here on out.

Since we've been discussing monetary proficiency, I thought I'd impart a statement to you that I see as exceptionally rousing. It's by Benjamin Franklin, and it says, "An interest in information pays well."

I think this is a truly strong message, and it's one that I trust you'll recollect as you proceed to learn and develop.

In the event that you're keen on a more current interpretation of monetary proficiency, I suggest looking at something crafted by Suze Orman. She's a monetary guide and TV character that's truly enthusiastic about assisting individuals makes shrewd choices with their cash. She's composed various books on the subject, and she's likewise the host of a famous webcast. Her methodology is truly open, and she generally offers useful guidance that anybody can follow.

Something else to remember as you're finding out about cash is the possibility of independence from the rat race. Independence from the rat race is the point at which you have sufficient cash set aside that you can carry on with the existence you need without agonising over cash.

This could mean various things to various individuals, yet the key is to have sufficient cash to cover your essential requirements to say the very least. Like that, you can zero in on the things that truly make a difference to you, similar to your family, your wellbeing, and your interests.

One last thought I might want to leave you with is the significance of making a move. It's not difficult to peruse and find out about individual budgets; however it's a lot harder to incorporate that information in fact.

It's memorable vital that even little changes can have a major effect after some time. So don't get overpowered, simply start little and continue to push ahead. Progress, not flawlessness, is the objective.

Could it be said that you are prepared to begin making a move on your monetary objectives?

Ways Women Can Safeguard Their Monetary Prosperity

The following are plans to assist women with safeguarding their monetary prosperity:

- Set a spending plan and stick to it.

- Make a just-in-case account.

- Put resources into yourself and your abilities.

- Exploit worker benefits, as 401(k) coordinating.

- Search for the best arrangements on protection and different administrations.

- Keep away from motivation purchasing.

- Take care of obligations as quickly as time permits.

- Robotize investment funds and bill instalments.

- Have customary monetary check-ups.

- Keep great records of your spending and pay.

- Realise your financial assessment.

The following are 15 additional ways:

- Exploit representative stock buy plans.

- Arrange your compensation and advantages.

- Put resources into retirement accounts, similar to IRAs and Roth IRAs.

- Begin a side gig to procure additional pay.

- Search out monetary schooling assets.

- Lessen your everyday costs.

- Ensure you're capitalising on your medical coverage.

- Think about buying incapacity protection.

- Think about long haul care protection.

- Plan for surprising costs, similar to vehicle fixes or hospital expenses.

- Differentiate your speculations.

The following are additional thoughts:

- Think about disaster protection.

- Use Visas dependably.

- Survey your monetary objectives routinely.

- Plan for significant life altering situations, similar to marriage or having a child.

- Figure out the assessment ramifications of your monetary choices.

- Exploit free assets, as monetary classes or online courses.

- Assume command over your funds, instead of allowing them to control you.

- Construct a strong monetary establishment, beginning with the rudiments.

- Be an educated buyer.

- Continuously read the fine print.

 The following are 5 additional thoughts:

- Keep awake to-date on monetary news and patterns.

- Know about tricks and misrepresentation.

- Remain coordinated with your funds, and keep every one of your records in a single spot.

- Consider utilising a monetary counsellor or mentor to assist you with arriving at your objectives.

- Make it a point to request help on the off chance that you really want it.

Ways Women Can Make Monetary Arrangement

Here are ways for women to make a monetary arrangement:

- Begin with a reasonable vision of your objectives and needs.

- Track your ongoing pay and costs.

- Make a month to month spending plan and stick to it.

- Distinguish the assets you need to work with.

- Think about your gambling resistance.

- Save for crises and surprising costs.

- Ensure you're covered by health care coverage.

- Plan for retirement.

- Think about your family's requirements.

- Make an arrangement for your domain.

The following are 10 more:

- Ensure your ventures are expanded.

- Figure out the assessment ramifications of your monetary choices.

- Consider your protection needs.

- Plan for significant life altering situations, similar to school expenses or purchasing a home.

- Assess your credit report and score.

- Make a just-in-case account.

- Consider renegotiating your home advance or different obligations.

- Set up programmed reserve funds and bill instalments.

- Search for proficient guidance when required.

Here are a few additional thoughts:

- Survey your arrangement routinely and make changes on a case by case basis.

- Remain informed about changes in the economy and monetary business sectors.

- Try not to make profound choices about your cash.

- Be straightforward with yourself about your ways of managing money.

- Get everything rolling regardless of whether you have a lot of cash to work with.

- Lay out a backup stash before you begin effective financial planning.

- Try not to get too up to speed in pursuing the most recent patterns.

- Try not to allow your feelings to impede your choices.

- Make an obligation reimbursement plan.

- Focus on putting something aside for retirement over putting something aside for your kids' school.

- Find out about various venture choices.

- Exploit business supported retirement plans.

- Know about the expenses related to money management.

- Ensure you grasp the dangers and likely compensations of every speculation.

- Broaden your speculations across various resource classes.

- Consider working with a robo-consultant.

- Exploit charge advantaged accounts, similar to IRAs and 401(k)s.

Here are a few additional thoughts:

- Utilise a planning application or other web-based instruments to assist you with dealing with your funds.

- Set up a direct store into your investment account.

- Consider utilising a high return bank account.

- Practise saving all the time.

- Use applications that gather together your buys and store the distinction into investment funds.

- Consider a currency market record or testament of a store.

- Lay out a rainy day account and keep it fluid.

- Shield your monetary data from fraud.

Astonishing Ways Women Can Save

 We should begin:

- Put forth an objective for your investment funds.

- Save first, then, at that point, spend.

- Pay yourself first.

- Mechanise your reserve funds.

- Wipe out pointless costs.

- Dispose of memberships you don't utilise.

- Search for the best arrangements on bills.

- Use coupons and limits.

- Purchase in mass.

- Purchase nonexclusive brands.

- Stay away from drive-books.

- Make a rundown before you go out on the town to shop.

- Carry your lunch to work.

Here are a few additional thoughts:

- Get a flat mate.

- Think about scaling back your living space.

- Search for garments at secondhand shops.

- Fix as opposed to supplanting.

- Attempt the 30-day rule prior to making a buy.
- Exploit dependability programs.

- Get a library card and get books, motion pictures, and music.

- Exploit free or minimal expense diversion choices.

- Attempt Do-It-Yourself as opposed to paying for administrations.

Ways Women Can Contribute

- Begin a little.

- Exploit business supported retirement plans.

- Put resources into your wellbeing.

- Put resources into yourself.

- Mechanise your effective financial planning.
- Differentiate your speculations.

- Put resources into minimal expense list reserves.

- Consider minimising risk.

- Consider deadline reserves.

- Remain informed about the business sectors.

- Set a drawn out plan and stick to it.

- Survey your ventures occasionally.

- Try not to pursue profound choices.
- Show restraint.

Here are a few extra thoughts:

- Converse with a monetary consultant.

- Consider a singular retirement account (IRA).

- Research trade exchange reserves (ETFs).

- Consider charging advantaged accounts.

- Put resources into land.

- Put resources into your schooling.

- Add to your youngsters' school reserves.

- Take care of your obligation prior to effective financial planning.

- Remain trained and centred.

- Keep your speculation costs low.

- Know about tricks and misrepresentation.

Ways Women Can Bring in Cash Work For Them

Here are considerable ways women can bring in their cash work for them:

- Begin effective money management as soon as could be expected.

- Put resources into yourself (schooling, preparing, etc).

- Exploit charge advantaged accounts.

- Mechanise your reserve funds.

- Survey your ways of managing money.

- Look for the best arrangements on monetary items.

- Track your spending.

- Arrange your compensation.

- Put forth monetary objectives and work towards them.

- Plan for the unforeseen.

- Pay yourself first.

Here are a few additional ways:

- Try not to become involved with staying aware of the-Joneses trap.

- Continue finding out about cash and money management.

- Find support from a monetary guide or organiser.

- Search out coaches and good examples.

- Get your family engaged with your monetary preparation.

- Ponder your heritage and what you need to abandon.

- Converse with your loved ones about cash.

- Share your monetary information with others.

- Help other people accomplish monetary health.

- Remain informed about recent developments and what they mean for your funds.

- Realise your FICO assessment and attempt to further develop it.

- Monitor your credit reports and question any mistakes.

- Comprehend the rudiments of bequest arranging.

- Foster an arrangement for your retirement.
- Grasp the distinction between great obligation and awful obligation.

- Differentiate your speculations.

- Find out about the force of accumulating interest.

- Remain fixed on the long haul, even in the midst of financial vulnerability.

- Find out about money and what it can mean for your choices.

- Remain propelled by commending your monetary achievements.

There are bunches of extra ways of bringing in cash work for you, including:

- Limit your assessments by exploiting every accessible allowance and credits.

- Think about going into business or a part time job.

- Make a beneficial piece of your monetary arrangement.

- Exploit business benefits, for example, wellbeing bank accounts or 401(k) coordinating.

- Lay out a backup stash for startling costs.

- Investigate elective ventures, for example, land or shared loaning.

- Begin a 529 arrangement for your kids' schooling.

What about truly inventive ways of bringing in your cash work for you? Here you go:

- Trade for labour and products as opposed to utilising cash.

- Develop your own food to get a good deal on food.

- Utilise your abilities and gifts to bring in cash as an afterthought.

- Begin a side business on the web.

- Turn into a business visionary.

- Search for ways of adapting your side interests.
- Purchases utilised things rather than new.

- Make your home more energy-productive to save money on service bills.

- Reuse old things as opposed to purchasing new ones.

Chapter Four

Put Resources Into Your Future

For section four, we'll investigate the subject of putting resources into your future. With regards to effective financial planning, the key is to begin early and stay with it. Regardless of whether you're simply ready to contribute a modest quantity every month, the force of self multiplying dividends can have a major effect after some time.

Perhaps the main thing you can do to get ready for your future is to define monetary objectives and make an arrangement to accomplish them. This plan ought to incorporate both present moment and long haul objectives, as well as a technique for how you'll contact them. One of the most widely recognized monetary objectives is retirement.

With regards to putting something aside for retirement, there are a couple of key things to remember.

To begin with, begin as soon as possible, regardless of whether you can save a limited quantity every month.

Second, exploit any business supported retirement plans, for example, a 401(k) or 403(b), and contribute however much you can bear to.

Third, consider adding to a conventional or Roth IRA, which can give extra tax breaks.

At last, try to occasionally survey and change your retirement plan as your necessities and conditions change.

Besides putting something aside for retirement, there are alternate ways of putting resources into your future. One way is to begin a rainy day account.
This asset ought to be discrete from your standard investment account, and it ought to be utilised exclusively for crises, like unforeseen hospital expenses or an employment cutback.

Having a just-in-case account can give you true serenity and assist you with trying not to assume exorbitant premium obligation in case of a crisis. One more method for putting resources into your future is to put something aside for your kids' advanced degree. You can do this through a 529 arrangement, a Coverdell Schooling Bank account, or by setting up a different bank account.

One more significant method for putting resources into your future is to deal with your wellbeing. This can incorporate going with solid way of life decisions, like eating a nutritious eating routine and practising consistently. It can likewise incorporate dealing with your emotional well-being, which can assist you with being more useful and effective.

Likewise, it's vital to have sufficient protection inclusion, including wellbeing, life, and incapacity protection. At long last, consider setting up a bequest intended to safeguard your resources and accommodate your friends and family.

At long last, there are numerous ways of putting resources into your self-awareness and advancement.

This can incorporate taking classes, going to courses, understanding books, or tracking down a guide. Putting resources into your self-improvement can assist you with accomplishing your objectives and arrive at your maximum capacity. It can likewise assist you with being stronger and versatile despite change. In the present quickly impacting world, it's a higher priority than any time in recent memory to put resources into your self-improvement.

As well as putting resources into your self-improvement, putting resources into your relationships is likewise significant. Solid connections can offer help, solace, and a feeling of having a place. They can likewise assist you with accomplishing your objectives and explore life's difficulties.

Putting resources into connections can be essentially as straightforward as investing quality energy with friends and family, being a decent audience, and offering support. It can likewise include chipping in, joining a club or association, and partaking locally.

At long last, putting resources into your passions is significant. At the point when you accomplish something you love, you're bound to find lasting success and satisfaction. Finding your energy can take some time and investigation, yet it's definitely worth the work.

Far to find your energy incorporating difficult new things, taking a character test, or asking loved ones what they think your assets are. Whenever you've found your energy, set aside a few minutes for it in your life and seek after it with excitement and devotion.

Putting resources into your happiness is additionally significant. Research has shown that bliss is connected to better wellbeing, greater efficiency, and better progress.

You can put resources into your joy by rehearsing appreciation, setting reasonable assumptions, and investing energy in exercises that give you pleasure. Dealing with your psychological and actual wellbeing is likewise key to being blissful. So make a point to get sufficient rest, work-out routinely, and eat a solid eating routine.

Lastly, I might want to accentuate that putting resources into you isn't just about cash or material things.

It's likewise about putting resources into your self-improvement, connections, and interests. At the point when you centre on these things, you'll find that you have more energy, excitement, and euphoria in your life.

You'll likewise be stronger and ready to deal with anything that life tosses your direction. So recollect, putting resources into you is a venture that will pay off for a lifetime.

Is there something else you might want to be familiar with putting resources into yourself?

Something final I might want to make reference to is build interest. Accumulate revenue is the possibility that assuming you reliably put resources into yourself, the advantages will duplicate over the long haul. This can be valid for your funds, but at the same time it's valid for different parts of your life. For instance, assuming that you reliably put resources into your connections, they'll get more grounded after some time.

Furthermore, assuming you reliably seek after your interests, you'll track down additional bliss and satisfaction in your life. So recall, reliable and little speculations can amount to huge prizes.

Now that we've covered every one of the various ways of putting resources into yourself, I might want to pass on you with a couple of viable tips to begin. In the first place, put forth an objective and make an arrangement to accomplish it. This can be a little objective, such as perusing one book each month, or a bigger objective, such as beginning another profession. Then, separate your objective into little, attainable advances. At long last, be patient and praise your advancement en route. Keep in mind, putting resources into you is a deep rooted venture, not an objective.

I'd likewise prefer to leave you with a couple of updates about taking care of one. Try to focus on your wellbeing and prosperity, both genuinely and intellectually.

This incorporates eating a solid eating routine, getting sufficient rest, and setting aside a few minutes for unwinding and fun. Taking care of oneself is a significant piece of putting resources into yourself, and it can assist you with keeping focused with your objectives. At last, remember to rehearse self-sympathy. Be thoughtful to yourself and recollect that everybody has their faults and encounters mishaps.

Benefits Women Can Accomplish By Putting resources into Their Prospects

There are many advantages that women can accomplish by putting resources into their prospects. Here are only a couple:

- Expanded certainty and confidence.
- Further developed profession possibilities and pay potential.

- A feeling of direction and bearing throughout everyday life.

- Worked on by and large for wellbeing and prosperity.

- The capacity to seek after interests and interests.

- The capacity to have a beneficial outcome on the world.

- The capacity to set a genuine model for other people.

- A feeling of individual fulfilment and achievement.

- The information that you are in charge of your own future.

We should discuss another advantage - the capacity to reward others. At the point when you put resources into yourself, you are helping yourself, yet you are likewise helping other people.

You can utilise your insight and abilities to help other people accomplish their objectives, and you can utilise your assets to have a constructive outcome on the world. At the point when you put resources into yourself, you are genuinely having an effect on the existence of others. This can be amazingly fulfilling and satisfying.

One method for offering back is to turn into a tutor or good example for other people. You can impart your insight and experience to other people who are hoping to learn and develop. This can be an exceptionally remunerating experience, and it can likewise assist you with growing new abilities and bits of knowledge.

You can likewise offer back by chipping in your time or assets to a reason that means quite a bit to you. This could be anything from coaching youngsters to aiding fabricating houses for those out of luck.

There are such countless ways of offering in return, and it ultimately depends on you to find the ones that are generally significant to you.

One more significant part of putting resources into yourself is to gain from others. This implies searching out tutors, understanding books, going to studios, and gaining from your encounters. At the point when you are available to learn and develop, you will keep on growing your insight and abilities. This can prompt much more open doors and development. Keep in mind, nobody knows it all, and there is continuously a new thing to learn. The more you learn, the more you will actually want to accomplish.

Women, putting resources into your future is perhaps the main thing you can accomplish for yourself. It might appear to be overwhelming from the outset, yet the prizes are definitely justified. Begin by laying out little objectives and making little strides towards them.

When you begin getting results, you will be roused to keep putting resources into yourself. Keep in mind, the excursion is similarly all around as significant as the objective, so partake simultaneously and praise your achievements en route. In particular, be patient and kind to yourself. You merit the speculation!

I might want to leave you with one last thought. Putting resources into you isn't just about cash. It's tied in with putting resources into your physical, mental, and profound wellbeing. It's tied in with putting resources into your connections, your interests, and your self-improvement.

Putting resources into things makes you blissful and satisfied. So don't simply zero in on the dollars and pennies, yet additionally on the things that genuinely make a difference to you. No one but you can choose what those things are, so carve out an opportunity to reflect and sort out what makes the biggest difference to you.

What's in store Is Female

That is an enabling motto that has been utilised to rouse and urge ladies to assume command over their own lives and seek after their fantasies. The thought is that what's in store is loaded with conceivable outcomes, and ladies have the ability to shape it. What's in store is what we make it, and we can make a future that is comprehensive, different, and impartial for all.

Ladies are assuming an undeniably significant part in

moulding the world we live in, and this is something to be praised and energised. Along these lines, women, how about we assume responsibility for our prospects and make them what we maintain that they should be!

It's likewise critical to recall that what's to come isn't just about people, yet about society all in all. At the point when we put resources into ladies, we are additionally putting resources into the eventual fate of our networks, our nations, and the world.

Ladies are fundamental for the outcome of our general public, and when we put resources into their prosperity, we are generally good off. So we should cooperate to make a future that is brilliant, confident, and loaded up with a potential open door for everybody. How about we make the future female!

There are numerous ways that women can put resources into their fates. To start with, they can focus on their schooling and expert turn of events.

Second, they can find tutors and good examples who can

give direction and backing.

Third, they can define monetary objectives and foster an arrangement to accomplish them.

Fourth, they can zero in on their wellbeing and prosperity, both physical and mental.

At long last, they can reward their networks and have a beneficial outcome on their general surroundings.
These are only a couple of the numerous ways that women can put resources into their fates.

As you pursue your objectives, it's likewise vital to remain spurred and enlivened. One method for doing this is to learn about other fruitful ladies who have conquered difficulties and accomplished extraordinary things. These accounts can be a wellspring of motivation and can show that the sky's the limit assuming that you set your attention to it.

You can likewise find backing and consolation from different ladies who are on a similar excursion. There are numerous web-based networks and organisations that can offer this sort of help.

Significance of putting resources into your future

1. Ladies are critical to the progress of families, networks, and economies.

2. Ladies assume a crucial part in raising the up and coming age of pioneers.

3. Whenever ladies have financial open doors, they put resources into their families, youngsters, and networks.

4. Ladies' authority in business and legislative issues has been displayed to further develop execution and adequacy.

5. At the point when ladies approach training, they have a more prominent ability to decide and assume command over their lives.

6. Ladies are bound to put resources into their wellbeing and prosperity whenever they have monetary open doors.

7. Ladies' financial strengthening prompts more prominent orientation uniformity.

8. At the point when ladies have equivalent admittance to financial assets, it assists with diminishing neediness and craving.

9. Putting resources into ladies' schooling and preparing can assist with shutting the orientation pay hole.

10. Ladies' administration in associations prompts expanded development and imagination.

11. Ladies' monetary strengthening assists with decreasing orientation based viciousness.

12. Putting resources into ladies' financial strengthening can assist with lessening youngster marriage.
13. Ladies' monetary strengthening assists with making more steady and tranquil social orders.

14. Ladies' monetary strengthening has a far reaching influence that helps the whole local area.

15. Ladies are key drivers of financial development.

16. Ladies' monetary strengthening prompts better kid nourishment and wellbeing.

17. Ladies' financial strengthening assists with decreasing orientation disparity.

18. Ladies' monetary strengthening is vital to finishing outrageous neediness.

19. Putting resources into ladies' monetary strengthening emphatically affects the climate.

20. Putting resources into ladies' monetary strengthening can assist with shutting the orientation advanced partition.

How Women Can Put Resources Into Their Fates

1. Put forth monetary objectives and make an arrangement to accomplish them.

2. Construct your reserve funds and venture portfolio.

3. Put resources into your wellbeing and prosperity.

4. Put resources into your profession.

5. Foster your abilities and information.

6. Search out coaches and good examples.

7. Be a deep rooted student.

8. Go into business.

9. Engage locally.

10. Utilise your voice to advocate for change.

11. Deal with yourself genuinely and intellectually.

12. Make a strong organisation of loved ones.

13. Have confidence in yourself and your capacities.

14. Face challenges and challenge yourself.

15. Be relentless and don't surrender.

16. Be patient and keep fixed on your objectives.

17. Deal with your actual wellbeing.

18. Develop an inspirational perspective and point of view.

19. Encircle yourself with positive individuals.

20. Carry on with a healthy lifestyle and set aside a few minutes for the things that fulfil you.

Keep in mind; these are only a couple of thoughts. There are numerous alternate ways of putting resources into your future.

Reasons Women Ought To Put Resources Into Their Prospects

1. To have the option to monetarily deal with themselves and their families.

2. To fabricate a solid and agreeable future for themselves.

3. To be in charge of their monetary future.
4. To experience harmony of the brain and steadiness.

5. To have the option to seek after their interests and dreams.

6. To have the opportunity to pick how to carry on with their lives.

7. To have the ability to arrive at conclusions about their own lives.

8. To have the option to serenely resign.

9. To accommodate their youngsters' schooling and future.

10. To assist with shutting the orientation pay hole.

11. To assist with separating hindrances to ladies' progression.

12. To add to a more equivalent and just society.
13. To make the world a superior spot for people in the future of ladies.

14. To move different ladies to put resources into their fates.

15. To decidedly affect their general surroundings.

16. To feel engaged and satisfied.

17. To accomplish a feeling of direction and importance

in their lives.

18. To have the option to leave an inheritance for their friends and family.

19. To have an effect on the planet.

20. To make an imprint that is significant and enduring.

21. To feel refined and pleased with their accomplishments.
22. To feel refined and pleased with their commitment to the world.

23. To have something to show for the entirety of their persistent effort and devotion.

24. To leave the world a preferred spot, they tracked it down.

25. To feel certain and confident.

26. To feel refined and happy with their life.

27. To have the option to think back on their existence with fulfilment.

Chapter Five
Organise Like a Boss

In part five, we'll investigate how to organize like a boss. Arranging is a significant ability that can assist you with getting what you need throughout everyday life. Whether it's arranging compensation, advancement, an agreement, or some other circumstance, having the option to haggle successfully is fundamental.

In this part, we'll cover the fundamentals of discussion, including how to get ready, how to utilise non-verbal communication and manner of speaking, and how to keep away from normal errors. We'll likewise investigate the specialty of influence and how to utilise it for your potential benefit.

To begin, understanding the fundamentals of negotiation are significant.

Exchange is a course of conversation and split the difference wherein at least two gatherings attempt to agree.

The objective of discussion is to accomplish a commonly useful result, where the two players leave feeling fulfilled. To haggle successfully, you want to have an unmistakable comprehension of what you need and what you're willing to provide to get it. You likewise should have the option to peruse the other party's non-verbal communication and manner of speaking, and to figure out their inspirations.

Now that we've covered the essentials, we should investigate a few explicit ways to arrange like a chief. The main tip is to get ready quite a bit early. Before you go into any exchange, you ought to set aside some margin to investigate the other party and grasp their objectives and inspirations. You ought to likewise have a reasonable thought of what you need to accomplish and what you're willing to surrender. Arrangement is critical to progress in any exchange.

The subsequent tip is to utilise non-verbal communication and manner of speaking for your potential benefit.

The subsequent tip is to utilise non-verbal communication and manner of speaking to convey certainty and authority. Stand upright, visually engage, and utilise a firm however deferential manner of speaking. This will assist you with projecting certainty and authority, which can be critical to getting what you need in a discussion.

You ought to likewise know about the other party's non-verbal communication and manner of speaking, and change your methodology appropriately. For instance, in the event that the other party appears to be anxious or reluctant, you might have to adopt a milder strategy.

The third tip is to be adaptable and ready to think twice about. No exchange is truly going to go the way you need it to, so it means quite a bit to provide something to get what you need. This doesn't mean you ought to quit any pretence of all that you need, yet it implies being available to hearing the other party's perspective and being willing to make a few concessions. Compromise is a fundamental piece of any effective discussion.

The fourth tip is to utilise the influential ability for your potential benefit. Influence is the craft of persuading somebody to do something by speaking to their inclinations and values.

In a discussion, you can utilise influence to get the other party to see your perspective and concur with your situation. To be powerful, you really want to grasp the other party's point of view and address their qualities and interests.

For instance, assuming the other party values proficiency, you can engage that by bringing up how your proposition will set aside time and cash.

The fifth tip is to constantly remain proficient and conscious. Dealings can be upsetting and profound, however keeping a degree of incredible skill and regard during the process is significant.

This implies utilising proper language, being thoughtful

of the other party's time, and keeping away from individual assaults. Regardless of whether the other party is being absurd, you ought to constantly stay under control and stay aware. This will assist with keeping the discussion on target and keep it from crashing.

The 6th tip is to know when to leave. Once in a while, regardless of how diligently you attempt, you will not have the option to agree with the other party.

For this situation, it's vital to know when to leave and not burn through any additional time or energy on a waste of time. Leaving a discussion can be troublesome, yet it's generally expected to be the best thing to do. Keep in mind, few out of every odd exchange merits winning, and in some cases the best result is to end it nimbly and continue on.

The seventh and last tip is to constantly trail behind a discussion. This implies sending a subsequent email or letter saying thanks to the next party for their time and repeating any arrangements that were made. This is a basic yet significant step that can assist with hardening the consequences of the exchange and guarantee that everybody is in total agreement. It's likewise an extraordinary chance to construct a positive relationship with the other party, which can be helpful later on.

One final idea before we wrap up - recollect that careful discipline brings about promising results. The more you arrange, the better you'll become at it. So make sure to take on dealings, regardless of their they're beyond your usual range of familiarity. You'll learn and develop as you go, and you'll be flabbergasted at the amount you can accomplish when you set your attention to it.

While we're on the subject of development, I might want to raise the possibility of "development attitude." This is the conviction that your capacities and knowledge are not fixed and can be created over the long haul. With a development mentality, you'll be bound to take on new difficulties and to gain from your mix-ups. This is the ideal attitude to have while arranging, since it will permit you to remain liberal and versatile.

Each woman ought to figure out how to arrange like a chief, since a significant expertise can help you in all parts of your life. From professional success to individual connections, exchange abilities can have a major effect.

Figuring out how to arrange can assist you with getting what you need and need, while keeping up with deference and nobility. It can likewise assist you with building positive connections and make a seriously satisfying life. In this way, in the event that you're not currently a specialist mediator, now is the right time to begin!

One last remembered to leave you with - remember to praise your triumphs! Discussion is difficult work, and when you've accomplished something incredible, it means a lot to pause for a minute to recognize your achievement. This won't just lift your certainty, yet it will likewise persuade you to continue developing and working on your abilities.

So feel free to applaud yourself - you merit it!

Discussion Abilities for Women

Here are some particular discussion abilities that can be especially valuable for ladies:

- Request what you need straightforwardly, without being excessively forceful.

- Practise undivided attention and be interested about the other party's viewpoint.

- Use "I" articulations to communicate your own necessities and needs.

- Know your value and backer for yourself.

- Remain mentally collected under tension and don't think about things literally.
- Stay liberal and adaptable, while being clear about your needs.

Expanding on that last point, it's vital to know your value and to advocate for yourself. This implies having an unmistakable comprehension of what you offer that would be useful and what you merit. At times, this can be trying for ladies, who might be associated with putting others' necessities in front of their own. Be that as it may, when you haggle from a position of self-esteem and self-promotion, you're bound to obtain the result you need.

Another expertise that is especially significant for ladies is the capacity to haggle for other people. Ladies frequently end up in the job of supporting other people, whether it's their youngsters, partners, or clients. In these circumstances, it's vital to have areas of strength for some time actually keeping up with deference and compassion.

Having the option to adjust these two things is an exceptional and strong expertise that can be truly important in various settings.

One final discussion expertise that is particularly helpful for ladies is the capacity to haggle in a social scene. Ladies are frequently associated to work in gatherings and to team up with others. This can be a benefit with regards to exchange, as it takes into consideration numerous points of view and can prompt a more inventive and compelling arrangement. In the event that you're in a social scene, try to pay attention to everybody's feedback and to stay conscious of varying conclusions.

Discussion Best Practices for Women

Here are some discussion best practices for ladies:

- Center on connections, in addition to the result.
- Know your own qualities and needs.

- Figure out the other party's necessities and interests.

- Adopt a cooperative strategy.

- Be available to intelligent fixes.

- Keep an inspirational perspective and a funny bone.

These prescribed procedures can assist you with accomplishing the most ideal result in any discussion circumstance.

Presently, we should discuss some normal exchange slip-ups to stay away from.

To begin with, don't make suppositions about the other party's intentions or objectives. This can prompt miscommunication and a breakdown in the exchange cycle.

Second, don't take a "win-lose" approach, where you're just centred on getting everything you could possibly want.

Third, don't disregard your feelings or attempt to stifle them. Recognizing your feelings can really assist you with pursuing better choices.

At last, don't get impeded in the subtleties and neglect to focus on the master plan.

As well as staying away from these mix-ups, there are

additionally a few explicit methodologies that can assist you with capitalising on your talks. One system is to utilise the "I feel" strategy. This includes communicating your feelings without accusing the other party. For instance, rather than saying "You caused me to feel awful when that's what you said," you could say "I felt upset when that's what you said." This procedure can assist you with imparting your sentiments in a useful and non-fierce manner.

Another procedure is to utilise the "misting" strategy. This includes recognizing the other party's viewpoint without tolerating or dismissing it. For instance, you could say "I comprehend the reason why you could feel as such" or "I can perceive how that is a significant issue for you." This method can assist with diffusing pressure and keep the discussion pushing ahead.

At long last, it's essential to utilise "enchantment words" to keep the discussion on target. These incorporate words like "and," "however," and "if." These words can assist you with overcoming any barrier between two restricting thoughts or viewpoints. They can likewise assist you with proposing a split the difference or settle on some shared interest. Have you at any point saw how strong these words can be in an exchange?

How Women Can Organise Like a Boss

The following are different ways that women can become effective moderators:

1. Know your value and worth.

2. Be emphatic and certain.

3. Properly investigate things and plan.

4. Pay attention to the next party's viewpoint.

5. Extend regard and sympathy.

6. Be clear and compact in your correspondence.

7. Adopt a cooperative strategy.

8. Request what you need.

9. Be adaptable and open to think twice about.

10. Leave if important.

11. Try not to think about things literally.

12. Keep cool-headed and proficient.

13. Try not to allow feelings to cloud your judgments.

14. Use humour when proper.

15. Remain positive and arrangement centred.

16. Show appreciation and appreciation.

17. Fabricate areas of strength for help.

18. Get outside input and guidance.

19. Face challenges and gain from your errors.

20. Be patient and constant.

21. Don't hesitate for even a moment to haggle for you.

22. Try not to underrate yourself.

23. Be valid and consistent with you.

24. Have confidence in yourself and your capacities.

Significance

The following are 20 justifications for why women really should arrange like a chief:

1. To close the orientation pay hole.

2. To acquire regard in the working environment.

3. To be viewed as an equivalent and esteemed colleague.
4. To have a voice and impact in the working environment.

5. To accomplish professional success.

6. To feel more satisfied and fulfilled in your vocation.

7. To set a positive model for different ladies.

8. To rouse others to accomplish their objectives.

9. To be a good example for people in the future.

10. To order more significant compensations.

11. To acquire what you're worth.

12. To have the independence from the rat race to seek after your fantasies.

13. To be monetarily secure and free.

14. To have the option to help your loved ones.

15. To have more prominent monetary security.

16. To create generational financial momentum.

17. To have more command over your funds.

18. To accomplish a better quality of living.

19. To have the option to reward your local area.

20. To carry on with an existence of direction and

significance.

Nuts and bolts

The following are nuts and bolts of exchange for women:

1. Know your objectives and what you're willing to surrender.

2. Be ready and know your realities.

3. Tune in and sympathise with the other party.

4. Hold your feelings in line.

5. Keep cool-headed and proficient.

6. Keep in touch.

7. Keep your non-verbal communication open and positive.

8. Use "I" proclamations rather than "you" explanations.

9. Try not to utilise absolutes like "consistently" or "never".

10. Be clear and succinct.

11. Know about your manner of speaking.

12. Be adaptable and open to think twice about.

13. Be decisive, yet not forceful.

14. Persevere when suitable.

15. Leave if important.

16. Go ahead and request what you need.

17. Try not to apologise superfluously.

18. Take as much time as is needed and don't rush the cycle.

19. Make sure to inhale and remain loose.

20. Remain positive and hopeful.

Could it be said that you are having good expectations about your capacity to arrange?

Instructions to Plan To Organise Like A Boss

You have it! The following are 15 methods for getting ready for a fruitful discussion:

1. Research the other party and the circumstance.

2. Expect the other party's necessities and interests.

3. Set up a rundown of your needs and objectives.

4. Contemplate your "primary concern.
5. Record a couple of key ideas.

6. Practise your discussion abilities with a companion or relative.

7. Dress suitably and project certainty.

8. Get a decent night's rest and have a solid breakfast.

9. Show up before the expected time and set up the actual space.

10. Set the vibe with a well disposed hello.

11. Begin the discussion with an optimistic outlook.

12. Keep in touch and utilize positive non-verbal communication.

13. Listen cautiously and take notes.

14. Be patient and take as much time as necessary.
15. Make sure to request explanation or rehash data.

In the event that you follow these tips, you'll make certain to have a useful and effective exchange.

Step by step instructions to Utilise Non-verbal communication and Manner of speaking

Without a doubt! Here are ways to utilise non-verbal communication and manner of speaking for your potential benefit:

1. Keep a loose and upstanding stance.

2. Utilise open and inviting non-verbal communication.

3. Visually connect and grin.

4. Keep your hands and arms open and loose.

5. Keep your signals deliberate and certain.

6. Try not to fold your arms or legs.
7. Utilise a strong handshake.

8. Talk with an unmistakable and quiet voice.

9. Utilise positive and perky language.

10. Utilise undivided attention abilities.

11. Try not to hinder or talk over the other party.

12. Take brief delays to let your message hit home.

13. Differ your tone and emphasis.

14. Keep an impartial or inspirational vibe.

15. Use reflecting to construct compatibility.

16. Attempt to match the other party's speed and energy.

17. Control your breathing and vocal volume.

18. Use stops to add accentuation.

19. Utilise your voice to convey energy.

20. Reflect the other party's non-verbal communication to assemble compatibility.

Normal Slip-ups To Keep away from

The following are 20 normal slip-ups to stay away from during exchange:

1. Neglecting to get ready.

2. Hurrying the interaction.

3. Zeroing in on winning, not tracking down an answer.
4. Making suspicions.

5. Lacking certainty.

6. Showing up too anxious to even consider satisfying.

7. Giving in too without any problem.

8. Neglecting to effectively tune in.

9. Blowing your top.

10. Losing your awareness of what's actually funny.

11. Turning out to be excessively protective.

12. Permitting feelings to dominate.

13. Making individual assaults.

14. Lying or being dishonest.

15. Misrepresenting or limiting realities.

16. Giving ultimatums.

17. Being excessively obstinate.

18. Lacking admiration.

19. Neglecting to keep up with proficient limits.

20. Neglecting to keep your word.

By staying away from these normal slip-ups, you'll be well headed to turning into a gifted mediator.

Involving The Craft of Influence In Exchange

The following are 20 ways to involve the craft of influence in discussion:

1. Fabricate compatibility and trust.

2. Grasp the other party's viewpoint.

3. Recognize shared interests.

4. Use rationale and realities to help your contentions.

5. Appeal to the next party's feelings.

6. Use stories and tales to represent your focus.

7. Present your defence utilising relationships.

8. Pose unconditional inquiries.

9. Make it individual.

10. Utilise encouraging feedback.

11. Lay out a need to get moving.

12. Use shortage and selectiveness for your potential benefit.

13. Influence the force of correspondence.

14. Appeal to the next party's feeling of reasonableness.

15. Recognize the other party's concessions.

16. Make little demands first.

17. Use differences to feature your advantages.

18. Go through friendly confirmation to back your cases.

19. Appeal to the next party's awareness of certain expectations.

20. Get the other party to sincerely commit a public responsibility.

Ways Women Can Haggle For More significant pay

Here are a few procedures to assist you with haggling for a more significant compensation:

- Properly investigate things.

- Know your value.

- Practise your pitch.

- Be certain and decisive.

- Plan for protests.
- Request what you need.

- Try not to apologise.

- Center around your worth.

- Feature your achievements.

- Be ready to leave.

- Try not to acknowledge the main deal.

- Show your excitement.

- Remain positive.

- Request input.

- Use non-verbal communication that conveys certainty.

- Be proficient.

- Practise undivided attention.

- Seek clarification on pressing issues.

- Be adaptable.

- Present a mutually beneficial arrangement.

- Keep cool-headed and creative.

- Stress your extraordinary abilities and encounters.

- Utilise influential language.

- Construct compatibility.

- Be deferential.

- Hold your feelings within proper limits.

- Remain arrangement situated.

- Remain fixed on your objective.

- Be available to think twice about.

- Know when to end the discussion.

- Thank the other party.

- Archive the understanding.

I have a more to share:

- Make sure to arrange.

- Be amiable however firm.

- Try not to think about it literally.

- Feel free to request help.

- Show restraint.

- Make sure to leave.

- Trail not too far behind the exchange.

- Remain coordinated.

- Take notes during the discussion.

- Be ready to haggle again from here on out.

- Keep cool-headed and sure.

- Make sure to grin!

- Be ready to settle the negotiation.

Ways Women Can Haggle For Advancement

Here are a few hints:

- Know your value.

- Exhibit your worth.

- Be prepared to show your outcomes.

- Put forth clear objectives and goals.

- Be ready to shout out.

- Grandstand your abilities and accomplishments.

- Present areas of strength for yourself.

- Remain positive and expert.

- Show your energy and excitement.
- Understand what you need and request it.

- Be available to criticism and ideas.

- Be deferential and gracious.

- Be certain about your capacities.

- Adopt a cooperative strategy.

- Fabricate associations with key leaders.

- Use information to help your case.

- Feature your commitments to the organisation.

- Show how your advancement will help the organisation.

- Hold your feelings within proper limits.

- Try not to take "no" as the last response.
- Be ready to haggle once more.

- Have a contingency plan.

- Keep even-tempered and centred.

- Recollect that it's not private.

- Make sure to face a challenge.

- Be inventive and adaptable.

- Be clear about what you need.

- Be explicit about your solicitation.

- Be ready to think twice about.

- Listen cautiously to the next party.

- Know about your non-verbal communication.

- Remain positive and expert.

- Be ready to make a counteroffer.

- Be deferential and gracious.

- Be ready to leave.

- Be certain and decisive.

- Don't hesitate for even a moment to request something more.

- Show your appreciation.

Ways Women Can Haggle For Agreement

Here's are ways:

- Know your value.

- Have a reasonable comprehension of the agreement terms.

- Properly investigate things.

- Be ready to arrange.

- Be decisive and certain.

- Be proficient and considerate.

- Be patient and deferential.

- Use civility and discretion.

- Don't hesitate for even a moment to get clarification on pressing issues.

- Utilise the right language.

- Ensure you have a mutually beneficial mentality.

- Be clear about your assumptions.

- Be ready to think twice about.

- Know your main concern.

- Keep the discussion positive.

- Make sure to leave.

- Tune in.

- Underline the advantages of the agreement.

- Be adaptable and innovative.

- Be clear about your assumptions.

- Be clear about your necessities.

- Keep cool-headed and creative.

- Make sure to say no.

- Know when to yield.

- Be ready to haggle once more.

- Hold your feelings within proper limits.

- Know about the other party's non-verbal communication.

- Focus on the other party's nonverbal signs.

- Make it a point to request an explanation.

- Be straightforward.

- Assemble affinity with the other party.

- Zero in on what means quite a bit to you.

- Remain consistent with your qualities.

- Know about your tone and disposition.

- Remember to grin!

- Be aware of the other party's time.

- Tell the truth and be direct.

- Be ready to back up your cases.

- Make sure to leave.

- Be conscious of the other party's necessities.

- Make sure to request a break.

- Try not to think about things literally.

- Be clear about your objectives.

- Haggle with honest intentions.

- Be ready to think twice about.

- Attempt once more.

- Be available to intelligent fixes.

- Be ready to issue a settlement.

- Remain positive and hopeful.

- Keep fixed on the ultimate objective.

- Be liberal and ready to learn.

- Remain mentally collected under tension.

- Be certain about your capacities.

- Make sure to face challenges.

- Be imaginative and liberal.

- Buckle down.

- Be adaptable and versatile.

- Remain consistent with your qualities.

Ways Women Can Turn into A Specialist Arbitrator

Here are a few stages that can help anybody, including women, become a specialist moderator:

- Research the other party.

- Find out about the other party's requirements and interests.

- Listen effectively.

- Be aware and amiable.
- Be certain and decisive.

- Know when to think twice about.

- Utilise undivided attention abilities.

- Remain composed and positive.

- Keep a receptive outlook.

- Leave.

- Keep fixed on the objective.

- Proceed with reasonable courses of action.

- Stay away from suppositions and generalising.

- Remain adaptable and versatile.

- Be inventive and open to groundbreaking thoughts.

- Haggle with honest intentions.

- Keep a receptive outlook and learn.

- Keep an expert disposition.

- Use non-verbal communication that conveys certainty.

- Keep in touch.

- Utilise uplifting feedback.

- Show appreciation and appreciation.

- Keep dealings classified.

- Remember to grin!

- Dress fittingly for the circumstance.

- Set sensible assumptions.

- Keep even-tempered under tension.

- Know your main concern.

- Have a contingency plan.

- Show that you're willing to buckle down.

- Make concessions.

- Show that you're certain about your situation.

- Recognize the other party's commitments.

- Keep your funny bones.

- Remain hopeful and positive.

- Be clear and succinct.

- Use "I" articulations.

- Pose unconditional inquiries.

- Utilise undivided attention methods.

- Focus on nonverbal signs.

- Listen more than you talk.

- Show interest in the other party.

- Tell the truth and morals.

- Know about your own inclinations.

- Know about the other party's predispositions.

- Be ready to share data.

- Be available to exchange.

- Be fair and deferential.

- Figure out the other party's viewpoint.

- Show restraint.

- Be determined.

- Be ready to think twice about.

- Be clear about your assumptions.

- Try not to set expectations.

- Request explanation when required.

- Utilise positive language.

- Be certain and decisive.

- Put down stopping points.

- Grasp the other party's inspiration.
- Be ready to say "no."

- Keep the exchange pushing ahead.

- Request help.

- Stay away from individual assaults.

- Utilise a go between if essential.

How Women Can Haggle For Other people

To get everything rolling, remembering a couple of things is significant. You'll have to:

- Have a reasonable comprehension of the objectives of the individual you're haggling for.

- Have an unmistakable comprehension of the other party's objectives.

- Be a gifted communicator.

- Grasp the power elements at play.
- Be moral and legit.

- Split the difference.

- Leave if fundamental.

- Be patient and determined.

- Have areas of strength for any of the issues in question.

- Have profound information on the significant statistical data points.

- Ensure you have a strong handle of the significant regulations and guidelines.

- Be totally ready and efficient.

- Be adaptable and imaginative in your methodology.

- Be a decent audience.

- Know about social contrasts.

- Be aware of the other party.

- Know about your own predispositions and suspicions.

- Have a capacity for humour.

- Have an advanced feeling of sympathy.

- Be delicate to the next party's feelings.

- Fabricate affinity and entrust with the other party.

- Know about the other party's correspondence style.

- Be delicate to the power elements impacting everything.

- Have an unmistakable arrangement for the exchange.

- Face challenges.

- Stand firm.

- Make concessions.

- Make compromises.

- Be innovative and adaptable.

- Figure out something worth agreeing on.

- Be not entirely set in stone.

- Have an uplifting perspective.

- Stay zeroed in on the objective.

- Know about your nonverbal correspondence.

- Be clear and brief in your correspondence.

- Be well mannered and deferential.

- Be ready to address questions.

- Be clear about your needs.

- Be clear about your limits.

- Be clear about your assumptions.

- Be ready to say "no."

- Be ready to request what you need.

Chapter Six

Be Monetarily Arranged For The Unforeseen

A secret stash resembles a monetary security net - it's there to get you on the off chance that you come upon a difficult time or have a startling cost. Monetary crises can occur whenever, and it's vital to be ready for them. This part will assist you with figuring out how to make a backup stash, what to do assuming that you want to dunk into it, and how to revamp it whenever you've utilised it. You'll likewise find out about other monetary wellbeing nets like protection, investment accounts, and government benefits.

One of the main parts of being monetarily arranged for the startling is having a secret stash. A secret stash is a pot of cash that you've saved for surprising costs like hospital expenses, vehicle fixes, or an employment misfortune.

Specialists prescribe having no less than three to a half year of everyday costs saved in your secret stash. This might appear to be a ton, yet it's vital to have sufficient cash to cover your costs in the event that something occurs. The most effective way to construct a secret stash is to begin little and practice it regularly to save cash every month.

There are maybe one or two methods for making a rainy day account. One choice is to set up a different financial balance and move cash into it every month. You can likewise utilise a cash saving application or programmed move administration to save cash. Certain individuals like to keep their backup stash in real money, while others like to keep it in a high return investment account or a testament of store (Compact disc). It's critical to pick a protected spot to keep your secret stash that will procure you some interest while likewise being not difficult to get to when you want it.

One of the greatest advantages of enjoying a just-in-case account is harmony of the brain. Realising that you have cash saved to cover unforeseen costs can assist you with resting better around evening time. Furthermore, having a backup stash can assist you with trying not to stray into the red on the off chance that you have a monetary crisis. Obligation can be costly and challenging to take care of, so it's ideal to keep away from it if conceivable.

At last, a backup stash can assist you with trying not to need to settle on difficult decisions in an emergency. For instance, in the event that you have a health related crisis, you might have to pick either covering your hospital expenses or paying your lease or home loan.

A typical inquiry concerning crisis reserves is how much cash you ought to have saved. The response relies upon your extraordinary monetary circumstance, yet a decent guideline is to have three to a half year of everyday costs saved. This sum might differ depending upon your professional stability, wellbeing, family circumstance, and different elements.

In the event that you have steady work and great health care coverage, you might have the option to get by with 90 days of costs saved. On the off chance that you have a less protected work or wellbeing concerns, it's smart to have a half year of costs saved.

One of the main things to recollect about a rainy day account is that it's just for crises. It's anything but a slush reserve forget-always or shopping binges. In the event that you utilise your backup stash for non-crisis costs, you'll be left without a wellbeing net assuming something occurs. It means a lot to oppose the impulse to plunge into your secret stash for regular costs, regardless of whether you're struggling with making a decent living. In the event that you're battling with your funds, it's smart to search for ways of cutting your costs or increment your pay.

One normal inquiry regarding crisis reserves costs they ought to cover.

The short response is that your secret stash ought to cover any costs that are important to keep up with your wellbeing, security, and fundamental living requirements. For instance, your secret stash ought to cover things like food, safe house, utilities, and drugs.

Then again, your just-in-case account shouldn't cover things like attire, diversion, or extravagance. Another normal inquiry is the means by which to renew your rainy day account after you've utilised it. The most ideal way to do this is to make a financial plan and focus on saving.

One more significant thing to recall about crisis reserves is that they're not a substitute for protection. Protection is intended to shield you from major monetary debacles, while a backup stash is intended to cover minor monetary crises. On the off chance that you don't have protection, it's smart to get it before you begin putting something aside for a secret stash.

There are various sorts of protection you might require, contingent upon your conditions. A few normal kinds of protection incorporate medical coverage, collision protection, property holders or tenants protection, and extra security.

There are a couple kinds of medical coverage you might require.

The first is significant clinical protection, which assists cover the expense of significant clinical costs with loving hospitalisation and medical procedure.

The second is doctor prescribed drug inclusion, which helps cover the expense of physician endorsed prescriptions.

The third is dental protection, which helps cover the expense of dental consideration.

The fourth is vision protection, which helps cover the expense of eye tests and glasses or contacts. It's essential to figure out the various sorts of medical coverage and pick the well conceived plan for your requirements.

Collision protection is one more significant kind of protection. It helps cover the expense of fixes or substitution assuming your vehicle is harmed or taken. There are a few distinct sorts of accident coverage, yet the most widely recognized are impact, thorough, and obligation inclusion. Impact inclusion helps pay for the expense of fixes in the event that you're in a mishap.

Far reaching inclusion helps pay for the expense of fixes on the off chance that your vehicle is harmed by some different option from a mishap, similar to a catastrophic event or burglary.

Risk inclusion assists cover the expense of harms or wounds you cause to others while driving.

One more significant sort of protection is property holders or leaseholders protection. This sort of protection helps cover the expense of fixing or supplanting your home or possessions assuming that they're harmed by fire, burglary, or one more covered occasion.

Mortgage holders protection additionally gives risk inclusion, which assists cover the expense of wounds or harms you with causing others while on your property.

Tenant protection is like mortgage holders protection,

yet it's particularly intended for individuals who lease their homes. Having the right sort of protection for your everyday environment is significant.

One more sort of protection to consider is extra security. Life coverage gives monetary assurance to your friends and family in case of your demise.

There are two fundamental kinds of extra security: term disaster protection and extremely durable extra security. Term life coverage gives inclusion to a particular time frame, similar to 10 or 20 years. Long-lasting disaster protection gives inclusion to your whole life. Picking the right sort of disaster protection for your requirements and budget is significant. A few different kinds of protection incorporate inability protection, long haul care protection, and umbrella protection.

Handicap protection is one more significant kind of protection. It replaces your pay in the event that you can't work because of a handicap. This kind of protection is particularly significant on the off chance that you have some work that is genuinely requesting or that expects you to be healthy.

Long haul care protection helps pay for the expense of long haul care, like nursing home consideration or in-home help. Umbrella insurance is a kind of protection that gives additional obligation security far in excess of what your other protection contracts give.
It's a discretionary kind of protection, yet it very well may be useful assuming that you have critical resources for safeguarding.

Another sort of protection to consider is pet protection. Pet protection helps cover the expense of veterinary consideration for your pet. It very well may be particularly helpful in the event that your pet has a constant condition or on the other hand assuming that they need crisis care. Some pet insurance contracts additionally cover routine considerations like inoculations and check-ups. Whether pet protection is ideal for you relies upon various elements, including the soundness of your pet and your financial plan.

One more sort of protection to know about is travel protection. Travel protection safeguards you monetarily assuming something turns out badly while you're voyaging. This could incorporate things like excursion crossing out, lost or deferred gear, and health related crises.

Whether you really want travel insurance relies upon various elements, including your objective, the length of your outing, and what your other protection contracts cover.

Now that we've covered a portion of the various sorts of insurance, we should discuss how to pick the right protection contract. The initial step is to figure out what your necessities are. Ponder what you need to safeguard and what dangers you're generally stressed over. When you know your requirements, you can begin looking at strategies.

There are a couple of things to remember while looking at strategies, including the expense, the inclusion, and the standing of the insurance agency. It's additionally essential to ensure you see any avoidances or restrictions in the approach.

Something final to remember is the significance of perusing the fine print. This is particularly significant with regards to insurance contracts, as they can be extremely intricate records. Before you sign any arrangement, ensure you see every one of the agreements. Assuming you're uncertain about something, ask your protection specialist or agent for an explanation. It's likewise smart to look around and get statements from different organisations before you go with a choice.

Now that we've covered a ton of the fundamentals of protection, I need to discuss probably the most well-known protection legends. One normal legend is that protection is excessively costly. While the facts confirm that protection can be a massive cost, it's likewise essential to consider the monetary security it gives.

Another legend is that you possibly need protection assuming you have a great deal of resources for safeguard.

While the facts confirm that protection is generally significant for individuals with huge resources, it's as yet smart for everybody to have some degree of inclusion.

Another normal protection fantasy is that getting a reasonable setup on insurance is unimaginable. While it is actually the case that insurance can be costly, there are exciting cash saving tips for your payments. For instance, you can analyse statements from numerous organisations, search for limits, and ensure you're not over insured.

Another fantasy is that you don't require protection

assuming you're sound. While the facts really confirm that sound individuals have a lower hazard of becoming ill, they can in any case profit from having protection in the event of a mishap or startling sickness.

Another normal legend is that you can't change your insurance whenever you've bought a contract.

This isn't correct - you can as a rule change your insurance whenever, as long as you follow the provisions of your contract. For instance, you might have the option to change your inclusion levels or add new inclusion assuming your requirements change.

Another fantasy is that it's not worth the effort to get protection assuming that you have a prior condition. While it is actually the case that previous circumstances can make it more challenging to get protection, there are choices accessible.

Another legend I need to discuss is that insurance agencies are on a mission to get you. While the facts really confirm that insurance agencies are organisations and they need to create a profit, it isn't actually the case that they are on a mission to trick you.

As a matter of fact, most insurance agencies have a great deal of shields set up to safeguard their clients.

For instance, most states have guidelines set up to ensure that insurance agencies are working reasonably.

Another normal misinterpretation is that all protection is something similar. This isn't correct - there are various kinds of protection, and everyone is intended to cover an alternate sort of chance. For instance, health care coverage is intended to take care of the expenses of clinical consideration, while extra security is intended to give monetary assurance to your family in the event that you bite the dust. Indeed, even inside each kind of protection, there are various degrees of inclusion and various choices accessible. In this way, it's vital to comprehend the distinctions before you purchase a strategy.

Tips How Women Can Get ready For Surprising

The following are 20 ways to get ready for the unforeseen:

1. Begin a rainy day account.

2. Have an arrangement for clearing or sanctuary in the event of a cataclysmic event.

3. Know your neighbourhood crisis methodology and assets.

4. Have an emergency treatment pack and essential clinical supplies close by.

5. Have an arrangement for how to contact loved ones in a crisis.

6. Have an arrangement for really focusing on pets and different wards in a crisis.
7. Have duplicates of significant archives, for example, insurance contracts, birth testaments, and monetary records.

8. Have a home stock of your assets.

9. Keep significant things in a protected, open spot.

10. Have a first aid pack with food, water, and different supplies.

11. Consider getting a generator or elective power source.

12. Keep your vehicle's fuel tank to some extent half full.

13. Master fundamental crisis abilities, like CPR and emergency treatment.

14. Get to know your neighbours and make a local area encouraging group of people.

15. Have a fall back for childcare, transportation, and other fundamental administrations.

16. Remain informed about nearby and public crises.

17. Be ready to clear or set up if important.

18. Have an arrangement for your meds and other wellbeing needs.

19. Have an arrangement for your monetary necessities, for example, ensuring your bills are paid.

20. Keep your telephone charged and have a reinforcement power source, like a versatile charger.

Ways Of getting ready For The Unforeseen

1. Really take a look at your insurance contracts to ensure you're covered.

2. Store significant records and resources in a protected spot.

3. Make a rundown of crisis contacts.
4. Make an arrangement for your pets.

5. Make an arrangement for really focusing on older or impaired relatives.

6. Make a family correspondence plan.

7. Know where to find crisis covers in your space.

8. Have an arrangement for dealing with pressure and

tension in a crisis.

9. Practice drills with your family or family.

10. Ensure you have a debacle supply unit with food, water, and different basics.

11. Know how to stop utilities, like water, gas, and power.

12. Secure your home by introducing window and entryway locks, and managing trees and hedges around your property.

13. Know about neighbourhood perils, like floods, storms, and fierce blazes.

14. Ensure your smoke and carbon monoxide locators are working.

15. Remain informed about weather patterns and

different crises.

16. Take a medical aid and CPR class.

17. Know about tricks that might emerge during a crisis.

18. Have an arrangement for your business, on the off chance that you're an entrepreneur.
19. Consider getting a generator or other back-up power source.

Reasons Women Ought to Plan For The Unforeseen

The following are 20 motivations to get ready for the unforeseen:

1. It's smarter to be protected than sorry.

2. You'll enjoy the harmony of the brain.

3. It can set aside your cash over the long haul.

4. It can save you time and bother.

5. It can assist you with keeping away from pressure and nervousness.

6. It can assist you with feeling more in charge.

7. It can assist you with being a decent good example for other people.

8. It can assist you with resting better around evening time.

9. It can assist you with keeping cool-headed and centred in a crisis.

10. It can assist you with dealing with the individuals who rely upon you.

11. It can assist you with feeling ready for anything that comes your direction.

12. It can assist you with getting past difficult stretches with flexibility.

13. It can assist you construct associations with the people who can help you in a crisis.

14. It can assist you with feeling more associated with your local area.

15. It can assist you with being more independent.

16. It can assist you with mastering new abilities and information.

17. It can provide you with a feeling of achievement.

18. It can assist you with feeling more enabled.

19. It can assist you with finding new interests and interests.

20. It can assist you with valuing the easily overlooked details throughout everyday life.

21. It can assist you with feeling more free and independent.

22. It can assist you with fostering a feeling of direction and importance.

23. It can assist you with turning out to be stronger and versatile.

24. It can assist you with feeling more in charge of your life.

25. It can assist you with taking full advantage of surprising open doors.

26. It can assist you with tracking down savvy fixes to issues.

27. It can assist you with feeling more ready to confront what's to come.

Significance Why Women Ought to Get ready For The Unforeseen

Here are a few motivations behind why ladies must plan for the unforeseen:

1. Ladies are bound to be single guardians.

2. Ladies are bound to be guardians for youngsters, older family members, or individuals with disabilities.

3. Ladies are bound to be essential providers in their families.

4. Ladies are bound to confront monetary difficulty in case of an emergency.

5. Ladies are bound to encounter aggressive behaviour at home and misuse.

6. Ladies are bound to confront segregation in the work environment.

7. Ladies are bound to encounter a compensation hole.

8. Ladies are bound to encounter orientation based viciousness in struggle zones.

9. Ladies are bound to encounter sexual viciousness.

10. Ladies are bound to confront hindrances to getting to

schooling and medical services.

11. Ladies are bound to encounter an absence of admittance to fundamental requirements like food, water, and sterilisation.

12. Ladies are bound to be affected by environmental change.

13. Ladies are bound to encounter removal because of contention or catastrophic events.

14. Ladies are bound to encounter dealing and sexual double-dealing.

15. Ladies are bound to be impacted by equipped struggle and different types of viciousness.

16. Ladies are bound to encounter basic liberties infringement.

17. Ladies are bound to encounter neediness.

18. Ladies are bound to be impacted by political flimsiness.

19. Ladies are bound to encounter hurtful conventional practices like early marriage and female genital mutilation.

20. Ladies are bound to be impacted by friendly and social standards that keep them from arriving at their maximum capacity.

Chapter Seven

Assume responsibility For Your Obligation

Obligation is an ordinary piece of life for some individuals, yet it can without much of a stretch winding crazy in the event that is not overseen as expected. This section will assist you with understanding your obligation, track down ways of decreasing it, and figure out how to try not to venture into the red in any case.

You'll find out about various kinds of obligations, how to focus on and pay down your obligations, and what to do on the off chance that you can't make your instalments.

Toward the finish of this section, you'll be prepared to assume responsibility for your obligation and make an arrangement to escape obligation for good.

The most vital phase in assuming responsibility for your obligation is to comprehend what sort of obligation you have.

There are two primary sorts of obligation: gotten and unstable. Gotten obligation is supported by insurance, similar to a house or a vehicle. In the event that you don't make your instalments, the loan specialist can take the security. Uncollateralized debt isn't upheld by security, so the loan specialist can't take anything in the event that you don't make your instalments. MasterCard and doctor's visit expenses are instances of uncollateralized debt.

When you understand what sort of obligation you have, the subsequent stage is to focus on your obligations. You ought to begin by making a rundown of every one of your obligations, including the sum you owe, the loan cost, and the base instalment. Then, you ought to rank them arranged by significance. Begin with the obligations that have the most noteworthy loan fee, as these will cost you the most cash over the long haul. Then, focus on any obligations that have a punishment for late instalments. At last, check the base instalment out.

On the off chance that an obligation has a high last instalment, it could be direr to pay off than one with a lower least instalment.

Whenever you've focused on your obligations, you can begin to make an arrangement to take care of them. There are two principal techniques you can utilise: the snowball strategy and the torrential slide technique. The snowball strategy includes taking care of the littlest obligation first, while the torrential slide technique includes taking care of the obligation with the most elevated loan fee first.

The snowball technique is ideal on the off chance that you really want inspiration to begin, while the torrential slide strategy is ideal to set aside the most cash.

The ensuing stage is to make a monetary arrangement. A spending plan is an arrangement for how you will spend your cash. It ought to incorporate all your pay and every one of your costs, including your obligation instalments.

Assuming that your costs are higher than your pay, you'll have to track down ways of diminishing your spending. The most ideal way to make a spending plan is to utilise a planning instrument, similar to a web-based device or an application. When you have a financial plan, you can follow your spending and ensure you're keeping focused.

Since you have a financial plan and an arrangement to take care of your obligations, now is the right time to set your strategy in motion. The initial step is to set up programmed instalments for your obligations. This won't assist you with ensuring you ever miss an instalment and stay away from late charges. Then, you ought to begin making additional instalments on your most noteworthy needs. This will assist you with taking care of it quicker and set aside your cash over the long haul.

It's additionally vital to know about the close to home side of obligation. Many individuals feel disgrace, uneasiness, or responsibility about their obligation.

These sentiments can make it harder to make a move and escape obligation. It's memorable critical that obligation is a monetary issue, not an ethical fizzling. You are not a terrible individual since you have obligation.

One method for managing the close to home side of obligation is to rehearse self-sympathy. Self-empathy is the demonstration of being kind and understanding towards you. At the point when you commit an error or have a down outlook on your obligation, attempt to be caring to yourself. You can express things to yourself as "I'm putting forth a valiant effort" or "Committing errors is OK." Rehearsing self-empathy can assist you with feeling not so much pushed but rather more spurred to make a move.

One last way to deal with obligation is to look for help from others. Conversing with a companion, relative, or a monetary instructor can assist you with feeling not so much alone but rather more propelled to make a move.

It can likewise assist you with getting groundbreaking thoughts and techniques for dealing with your obligation.

The fact that you're in good company makes accepting at least for now that you're feeling overpowered by your obligation, memorable essential. A huge number of individuals all over the planet are managing obligations. There are numerous assets accessible to help you, including free or minimal expense guiding, online care groups, and taxpayer supported initiatives. The significant thing is to venture out and connect for help.

Now that we've covered a few systems for managing obligation, we should discuss forestall obligation later on.

The most effective way to forestall obligation is to live inside your means. This implies spending less cash than you procure. You can do this by following your spending, making a financial plan, and tracking down ways of lessening your costs.

One more method for forestalling obligation is to assemble a backup stash. A backup stash is a bank account that you can use to cover surprising costs, similar to vehicle fixes or doctor's visit expenses. It's ideal to have no less than three to a half year of everyday costs set aside. This will assist you with abstaining from venturing into the red when something unforeseen occurs.

Sorts of Obligations

There are various kinds of obligation, however the following are 10 of the most widely recognized:

1. Charge card obligation: This is an obligation that you owe on a MasterCard. Charge card obligation ordinarily has exorbitant loan fees, so it means quite a bit to take care of it quickly.

2. Clinical obligation: This is an obligation that you owe for clinical consideration, similar to clinic bills or specialist's visits. Clinical obligations can be challenging to pay off, particularly in the event that you don't have protection.

3. Understudy loan obligation: This is an obligation that you owe for your schooling, similar to educational cost and charges.

4. Car advance obligation: This is an obligation that you owe for a vehicle credit. Car advances normally have lower financing costs than MasterCard, yet it's as yet critical to take care of them at the earliest opportunity.

5. Contract obligation: This is an obligation that you owe for your home credit. Contracts regularly have lower loan costs than different sorts of obligations, yet they can in any case be challenging to pay off.

6. Individual advance obligation: This is an obligation that you owe for an individual credit, which is a sort of credit that you can use for any reason.

7. Business credit obligation: This is an obligation that you owe for a credit that you took out for your business. Business credits ordinarily have higher financing costs than different sorts of advances.

8. Payday credit obligation: This is an obligation that you owe to a payday bank. Payday credits ordinarily have exceptionally exorbitant loan fees and ought to be kept away from if conceivable.

9. Charge obligation: This is an obligation that you owe to

the public authority for neglected charges. Charge obligation can be hard to pay off, and it can prompt punishments and interest charges.

10. Utility obligation: This is an obligation that you owe for your utilities, similar to power, water, and gas. Utility obligation can be hard to pay off, and it can prompt help detachment.

As may be obvious, there are a wide range of sorts of obligations. On the off chance that you're battling with obligation, looking for help from a monetary counsellor or other professional is significant.

Significance of Just-in-case account For Women

1. A backup stash can assist you with trying not to stray into the red.

2. A secret stash can give you inner serenity.

3. A backup stash can assist you with paying for unforeseen costs, similar to vehicle fixes or doctor's visit expenses.

4. A rainy day account can assist you with keeping up with your way of life assuming that you lose your employment.

5. A secret stash can assist you with trying not to plunge into your retirement reserve funds.

6. A backup stash can assist you with paying for surprising travel costs.

7. A backup stash can assist you with taking care of the expense of a significant home fix.

8. A backup stash can assist you with taking care of the expense of a significant vehicle fix.

9. A backup stash can assist you with paying for a significant home machine fix.

10. A secret stash can assist you with taking care of the expense of a significant clinical cost.

11. A backup stash can assist you with taking care of the expense of a significant pet cost.

12. A secret stash can assist you with taking care of the expense of a significant lawful cost.

13. A secret stash can assist you with paying for the expense of significant schooling cost.

14. A backup stash can assist you with taking care of the expense of a significant duty bill.

15. A backup stash can assist you with taking care of the expense of a significant climate related cost, similar to a cataclysmic event.

16. A backup stash can assist you with taking care of the expense of a significant employment cutback.

17. A secret stash can assist you with taking care of the expense of a significant relationship change, similar to a separation or a separation.

18. A backup stash can assist you with taking care of the expense of a significant profession change.

19. A backup stash can assist you with taking care of the expense of a significant way of life change, such as moving to another city.

Step by step instructions to Try not to Stray into the red

The Following Are Methods for Trying Not To Venture Into The Red:

1. Spend short of what you procure.

2. Save for enormous buys.

3. Try not to utilise charge cards for ordinary costs.

4. Make a month to month spending plan and stick to it.

5. Use cash rather than Visas whenever the situation allows.

6. Take care of your bills on time.

7. Try not to get cash to support a way of life you can't manage.

8. Try not to live check to check.

9. Make an arrangement for taking care of any current obligation.

10. Try not to give companions or family culpability you access to burning through cash you don't have

Nothing bad can really be said about being liberal, yet it's essential to ensure you're not forfeiting your monetary security to satisfy others. Adhere to your spending plan and say no when fundamental. Your monetary wellbeing is a higher priority than keeping up appearances.

11. Fabricate a backup stash.

12. Save for retirement.

13. Search for the wellbeing rates on advances and MasterCard.

14. Get monetary guidance from an expert.

15. Instruct yourself about individual budgets.

16. Keep away from motivation purchasing.

17. Pay for huge buys with cash.

18. Try not to settle on monetary choices in light of feeling.

19. Dispose of memberships and enrollments you

needn't bother with.

20. Live inside your means.

It's essential that staying away from obligation takes time and exertion. Fire little and develop your monetary information and discipline over the long run.

Chapter Eight

Make Numerous Revenue Sources

Welcome to part eight! This section is tied in with making numerous revenue sources. The initial step is to recognize your abilities and gifts. What are you great at? What do you appreciate doing? When you understand what you're great at, you can begin pondering ways of adapting your expertise.

There are numerous ways of bringing in cash on the web, from offering carefully assembled products to giving counselling administrations. Whenever you've distinguished your abilities and potential revenue sources, now is the ideal time to begin. Fire a little and move gradually up.

The subsequent stage is to make an arrangement for producing different revenue sources. This might incorporate putting forth objectives, recognizing assets, and making a timetable.

For instance, if you need to begin a side gig selling handcrafted products, you'll have to lay out an objective for how much cash you need to make, track down a stage to sell your merchandise, and make a timetable for when you need to send off your business.

Make sure to be patient and sensible with your objectives. It requires investment to fabricate various revenue sources, and zeroing in on higher standards no matter what is significant. Try not to wear yourself out by attempting to do a lot immediately.

When you have an arrangement set up, now is the right time to get everything rolling. The way to progress is consistency and industriousness. It could be enticing to surrender in the event that you don't get results immediately, however the most important thing is to continue onward and not get deterred. Rome wasn't implicit a day, and your numerous revenue streams will not be by the same token. Simply continue to move forward and you'll ultimately arrive at your objectives.

The last step is to be available to new open doors and to continue to learn. The universe of pay age is continuously changing, so keeping awake to-date on the most recent patterns and strategies is significant.

Ways to make Numerous Floods Of Pay

The following are a couple of extra ways to make numerous revenue sources:

- Differentiate your revenue sources. Try not to depend on only one kind of revenue.

- Have a plan B. Things don't generally work out as expected, so it's essential to have a plan B on the off chance that something turns out badly.

- Feel free to fizzle. Disappointment is a piece of the growing experience, so don't allow it to prevent you from attempting new things.

- Monitor your advancement. It's essential to keep tabs on your development so you can see what's working and so forth.

One method for making numerous revenue streams simpler to oversee is to mechanise however much as could reasonably be expected. For instance, you can set up programmed instalments for your bills and ventures.

You can likewise utilise apparatuses like IFTTT (On the off chance that This, That) to mechanise specific assignments. For instance, you can set up IFTTT to consequently present your blog entries via web-based entertainment or to send you an instant message when you get another email. Via robotizing however much as could reasonably be expected, you'll save time to zero in on the things that make the biggest difference.

For instance, on the off chance that you're bad at accounting, you can recruit a menial helper to do it for you. Or on the other hand, in the event that you hate making illustrations for your blog, you can re-appropriate that errand to a visual planner. By rethinking errands, you can zero in on the things that you're great at and appreciate doing. This will make it simpler to make various revenue sources, and it will likewise assist you with being more useful and productive.

At last, try to remain persuaded. Making numerous revenue streams takes time and exertion, so remaining persuaded and zeroed in on your goals is significant.

One method for remaining propelled is to find a local area of similar individuals who are likewise keen on making various revenue sources. You can join online discussions or gatherings, or you can find a tutor or mentor who can assist you with remaining focused. Encircling yourself with positive, steady individuals will make the excursion more agreeable and fruitful.

Another tip is to commend your triumphs, regardless of how little. Regardless of whether you just arrive at a little achievement, find an opportunity to celebrate it. This will assist you with remaining roused and enlivened to continue onward.

The following are a couple of normal inquiries individuals have about different revenue sources:

Q: What number of revenue streams would it be a good idea for me to have?

A: There's no one size-fits-all response to this inquiry. It relies upon your objectives, your way of life, and your gamble resistance. Certain individuals are content with only a couple of revenue sources, while others might need to have a few. The significant thing is to track down the right equilibrium for you. Begin with a couple of revenue sources and find out how it turns out.
You can constantly add all the more later in the event that you need to.

Q: How much cash do I have to begin making numerous revenue sources?

A: Once more, there's no one size-fits-all response to this inquiry. It relies upon the revenue streams you pick. Some revenue sources, such as contributing to a blog, can be begun with next to zero cash. Others, such as beginning a business, may require a bigger speculation. The most ideal way to sort out how much cash you really want is to explore the revenue streams you're keen on and make a financial plan. This will assist you with deciding how much cash you want to begin.

Q: What are the most well-known botches individuals make while attempting to make various revenue sources?

A: There are a couple of normal errors individuals make while attempting to make various revenue sources. To begin with, they might attempt to do a lot immediately. It's essential to begin little and spotlight on each or two revenue streams in turn. Second, they may not show enough restraint. Building different revenue streams takes time, so it means a lot to be patient and not surrender too early. At last, they may not enhance their revenue streams enough. It's essential to have a blend of latent and dynamic revenue streams to make a maintainable pay.

Q: What are some capricious revenue streams that individuals might not have thought of?

A: There are numerous whimsical revenue streams that individuals might not have thought of. A few models include:

- Making an internet based course or digital book

- Independent composition or visual communication

- Outsourcing or selling on eBay

- Partner showcasing

- Remote helper administrations

- Leasing an extra room or vehicle

- Turning into an online entertainment powerhouse

These are only a couple of instances of eccentric revenue

sources. There are a lot more choices out there, so it merits investigating every one of your choices.

Q: What are the advantages of having numerous revenue sources?

A: There are many advantages to having numerous revenue sources. In the first place, it can give a monetary security net. Assuming one revenue stream evaporates, you'll in any case have others to return to.

Second, it can assist you with arriving at your monetary objectives quicker. With various revenue sources, you can set aside and put away more cash, which will assist you with arriving at your objectives sooner.

Third, it can give you greater adaptability. With different revenue sources, you can pick the ones that fit your way of life and timetable the best. At long last, it can give a feeling of safety and dependability.

Q: What are the dangers of having numerous revenue sources?

A: While there are many advantages to having numerous revenue sources, there are likewise a few dangers to consider.

To start with, it tends to be tedious to deal with different revenue sources.

Second, monitoring your pay and expenses can be troublesome.

Third, it may very well be not difficult to become overpowered or extend yourself excessively far. Fourth, there is dependably the gamble that at least one of your revenue streams could evaporate.

At last, there is the gamble that your different revenue streams could make charges or lawful complexities.

Q: Is it conceivable to have an excessive number of revenue sources?

A: It is possible to have such a large number of revenue sources, and this can prompt issues. At the point when you have an excessive number of revenue sources, it tends to be hard to monitor everything and to remain coordinated.

You may likewise observe that you are investing more energy dealing with your revenue streams than really bringing in cash. Also, you might observe that you can't zero in on any one revenue source and are not seeing the outcomes you need.

That being said, there is no rigid rule about the number

of revenue streams is too much. It relies upon the individual and their way of life, as well as how much investment they need to commit to dealing with their revenue sources. Certain individuals flourish with various revenue sources, while others might like to zero in on only a couple. At last, it ultimately depends on every person to conclude what turns out best for them.

While concluding the number of revenue streams to seek after, it's vital to think about your own objectives, assets, and chance resistance. You might need to begin with only a couple of revenue sources and find out how it turns out prior to adding more. It's additionally vital to recall that quality is a higher priority than quantity. One very much oversaw revenue stream can be more productive than a few ineffectively overseen ones.

One more element to consider is the potential for revenue stream immersion. This is the point at which the market for a specific revenue stream becomes oversaturated, making it hard to find success. For instance, there are currently many bloggers attempting to bring in cash from writing for a blog, so it's harder than at any other time to stand apart from the group. This is an interesting point while concluding the number of revenue streams to seek after.

One method for staying away from revenue stream immersion is to zero in on specialty markets.
By finding a particular specialty and offering some incentive to a little gathering, you can try not to contend with the majority. For instance, rather than publishing content to a blog about broad way of life points, you could zero in on a particular specialty like moderate living or vegetarian cooking.

Another methodology is to expand your revenue sources. This implies having a blend of latent and dynamic revenue sources, as well as a blend of various kinds of revenue sources. Along these lines, on the off chance that one revenue stream evaporates, you actually have others to return to. For instance, you could have a blend of rental pay, online deals, and counselling pay.

Ways Women Can Make Floods Of Pay

1. Begin a blog

2. Sell items on Etsy

3. Begin a YouTube channel

4. Do independent composition

5. Begin a webcast

6. Turn into a remote helper

7. Turn into a holistic mentor

8. Sell stock photographs

9. Accomplish visual computerization work

10. Take reviews on the web

11. Compose digital books

12. Accomplish record work

13. Accomplish information passage work

14. Sell high quality artworks

15. Sell utilised garments on the web

16. House sit or pet sit

17. Begin a locally established childcare

18. Turn into a guide

19. Show English on the web

20. Turn into an online entertainment director.

These are only a couple of the numerous ways women can make floods of pay. With a touch of examination, you can track down considerably more choices that fit your abilities and interests. Simply make sure to take things slow and zero in on each or two revenue streams in turn.

Disconnected Organisations Women Can Make And Bring in Cash

1. Bread kitchen

2. Individual gourmet expert

3. Beauty parlour

4. Nail salon

5. Canine strolling/pet sitting

6. Specialised canine care

7. Housekeeping

8. Vehicle enumerating

9. Task administration

10. Individual customer

11. Rub advisor

12. Yoga teacher

13. Dance teacher

14. Mentoring administration

15. Home association administration

16. Individual preparation

17. Party organiser

18. Providing food administration

19. Occasion organiser

20. Florist.

Motivations Behind Why Women Ought To Have Floods Of Pay

1. Monetary freedom

2. More choices throughout everyday life

3. Higher acquiring potential

4. Capacity to follow your interests

5. Monetary security

6. Flexibility in the midst of emergency

7. A model for other people

8. Opportunity to face challenges

9. Adaptability to make changes

10. Less pressure and stress

11. More command over your life

12. Diminished reliance on others

13. More certainty and confidence

14. Further developed critical thinking abilities

15. Better connections

16. Additional opportunity for loved ones

17. Better rest

18. Greater innovativeness

19. Expanded efficiency.

As may be obvious, there are many advantages to having different surges of pay. Besides the fact that it can affect your monetary security, however it can likewise further develop your general prosperity.

Chapter Nine

Practice Monetary Arranging regularly

In this section, we'll examine the significance of practising monetary arranging all the time. Monetary arranging can be troublesome, however it's significant for your drawn out monetary wellbeing. Very much like some other propensity, it requires investment and work to make it a piece of your day to day daily practice. Yet, when you do, you'll receive the rewards long into the future.

We should begin by examining what monetary arranging

really is.

Monetary arranging is the method involved with making a guide for your funds. This guide ought to incorporate your objectives, your ongoing monetary circumstance, and your arrangements for what's in store.

A decent monetary arrangement ought to be customised to your particular requirements and conditions. It ought to consider your pay, your costs, your obligation, your reserve funds, and your speculations. It ought to likewise think about your objectives, both present moment and long haul. Furthermore, it ought to be sufficiently adaptable to adjust to changes in your day to day existence, for example, work changes, family changes, or surprising occasions.

The most vital phase in making a monetary arrangement is to lay out certain objectives. These objectives ought to be explicit, quantifiable, feasible, important, and time-bound (Shrewd).

For instance, a Shrewd objective may be "to save $5,000 for a backup stash inside the following year." This objective is explicit (it's tied in with setting aside cash), quantifiable (you know the amount you want to save), feasible (it's a sensible sum to save), pertinent (a backup stash is significant), and time-bound (you've given yourself a cutoff time).

When you have your objectives, you really want to make a financial plan. A financial plan is a spending plan that assists you with distributing your pay to various classes, like lodging, food, transportation, and diversion.

While making your financial plan, it's vital to be practical and fair with yourself about your ways of managing money. Make certain to follow your costs for a couple of months so you can get a precise image of your spending.

When you have a financial plan set up, you can begin dealing with your investment funds plan. Your reserve funds ought to be essential for your financial plan, and you ought to attempt to save a specific sum every month.

It's likewise really smart to computerise your reserve funds by setting up programmed moves from your financial records to your investment account. Along these lines, you don't need to make sure to save every month; it happens consequently.

Since you have a spending plan and a reserve funds plan set up, now is the right time to begin dealing with your obligation. On the off chance that you have any obligation, you ought to focus on taking care of it at the earliest opportunity. Begin by making a rundown of every one of your obligations, including the loan fee and least instalment for everyone. Then, make an arrangement to take care of the obligation with the most noteworthy loan fee first. This is known as the "snowball technique" of obligation reimbursement. As you take care of every obligation, you'll let loose more cash to take care of the following one, etc.

One more significant part of monetary arranging is anticipating retirement. This is the kind of thing that you ought to begin contemplating as quickly as time permits, regardless of whether retirement appears to be far away.

You ought to likewise consider extra security while making your monetary arrangement. Extra security can assist with safeguarding your friends and family in case of your passing.

Lastly, remember to anticipate startling costs. These are costs that you don't expect, for example, vehicle fixes, hospital expenses, or home fixes. It's really smart to have a just-in-case account to cover these costs.

Plan to have sufficient cash in your secret stash to cover no less than three to a half year of everyday costs. Along these lines, you'll be ready for any startling costs that surface.

Monetary arranging is a continuous interaction that requires some investment and exertion. In any case, it's worth the effort to have an arrangement set up that assists you with arriving at your monetary objectives.

How About We Start By Examining What Accomplishing Monetary Security:

1. Financial arranging can assist you with having a safer outlook on your future.

2. **Putting something aside for objectives**: With a monetary arrangement, you can lie out and accomplish your investment funds objectives.

3. **Limiting monetary pressure**: Having an arrangement can assist you with having a less focused outlook on cash.

4. **Creating financial wellbeing**: A monetary arrangement can assist you with creating financial stability over the long haul.

5. **Getting ready for retirement**: You can utilise a monetary arrangement to get ready for retirement.

6. **Overseeing obligation**: An arrangement can assist you with dealing with your obligation all the more really.

7. **Safeguarding your loved ones**: An arrangement can assist you with accommodating your family in case of your passing or handicap.

8. **Making arrangements for crises**: A backup stash is a significant piece of a monetary arrangement.

9. **Grasping your choices**: Monetary arranging can assist you with understanding your choices and settle on informed choices.

10. **Putting something aside for training**: In the event that you have kids, you can utilise a monetary arrangement to put something aside for their schooling.

11. **Making arrangements for significant life altering events**: An arrangement can assist you with planning for significant life altering situations like marriage, having kids, or becoming jobless.

12. **Keeping up with your way of life**: An arrangement can assist you with keeping up with your way of life in retirement.

13. **Remaining coordinated**: A monetary arrangement can assist you with remaining coordinated and monitor your funds.

14. **Exploiting tax reductions**: A monetary arrangement can assist you with exploiting tax cuts and derivations.

15. **Taking advantage of your advantages**: In the event that you have benefits through your manager, an arrangement can assist you with capitalising on them.

16. **Safeguarding your resources**: An arrangement can assist you with shielding your resources from dangers like expansion, market instability, and unforeseen costs.

17. **Taking full advantage of your income**: A monetary arrangement can assist you with capitalising on your pay and boost your reserve funds.

18. **Getting ready for the unforeseen**: An arrangement can assist you with planning for the unforeseen, like employment misfortune, separation, or a significant disease.

19. **Making arrangements for long haul care**: An arrangement can assist you with getting ready for the chance of requiring long haul care from now on.

20. **Accomplishing true serenity**: A monetary arrangement can give you inner harmony, realising that you're ready for anything life tosses your direction.

I trust this data has been useful. Assuming that you have

some other inquiries regarding monetary preparation or its significance, if it's not too much trouble, go ahead and inquire. Meanwhile, here's a couple of extra tips that might be helpful:

- **Begin early** - The earlier you start the good you'll be.

- **Find support from an expert** - A monetary consultant can assist you with making an arrangement that is ideal for you.

- **Focus on it** - Focus on monetary preparation in your life.

- **Audit and update your arrangement** - Your arrangement ought to be assessed and refreshed consistently to ensure it's actually addressing your necessities.

- **Continue to learn** - Keep on teaching yourself about individual budgets. The more you know, the better prepared you'll be to settle on brilliant monetary choices.

- **Embrace change** - Be available to make changes to your arrangement as your life altering events.

- **Center around what you have some control over** - You have zero control over the economy or the securities exchange; however you have some control over your spending and saving propensities.

- **Show restraint** - Monetary arranging is a long distance race, not a run. Try not to get deterred in the event that you don't get results immediately.

- **Keep it basic** - Don't over complicate your arrangement. Keep it basic and simple to follow.

- **Have a fall back** - Things don't generally work out as expected, so it's critical to have a plan B set up.

- **Be straightforward with yourself** - Don't attempt to

imagine you have more cash than you improve at overseeing cash than you are. Be straightforward with yourself about your funds and your capacities.

- **Put forth sensible objectives** - Your objectives ought to be testing however feasible.
Try not to get yourself in a position for disappointment by laying out unreasonable objectives.

- **Be focused** - Adhere to your arrangement and finish your responsibilities. It's the best way to arrive at your objectives.

- **Try not to contrast yourself with others** - Everybody's monetary circumstance is unique. Try not to contrast yourself with others or feel constrained to stay aware of the Joneses.

- **Partake in the excursion** - Monetary arranging isn't just about arriving at your objectives. It's additionally about partaking in the excursion en route.

Carve out an opportunity to commend your advancement and partake in the rewards for so much hard work.

- **Have some good times** - To wrap things up, play around with it! Monetary arranging doesn't need to be an errand. Track down ways of making it pleasant and you'll be bound to stay with it.

That is all I have on monetary preparation, however assuming you might want to discuss anything more connected with cash, I'm glad to talk. I realise that cash can be an unpleasant theme, yet I trust I've had the option to assist you with feeling more sure and in charge of your funds. On the off chance that there's anything more I can assist with, if it's not too much trouble, let me know.

Tips About Monetary Preparation

The following are 25 hints about monetary arranging that are explicitly for women:

1. Know your monetary objectives.

2. Established a financial plan and stand to it.

3. Figure out your pay and costs.

4. Plan for startling costs.

5. Save for retirement.

6. Put away a rainy day account.

7. Put away your cash admirably.

8. Survey your advancement routinely.

9. Be aware of your FICO assessment.

10. Converse with a monetary counsellor.

11. Assume command over your funds.

12. Assemble your monetary information.

13. Stay away from motivation purchasing.

14. Track your spending.

15. Take care of obligations.

16. Think about your family's necessities.

17. Make saving programs.

18. Live inside your means.

19. Instruct your kids about cash.

20. Assemble various surges of pay.

21. Focus on your objectives.

22. Safeguard your resources.

23. Plan for life changes.

24. Remain positive and spurred.

25. Commend your triumphs.

These tips ought to assist you with making a strong monetary arrangement that works for you.
Keep in mind, beginning anticipating your future is rarely past the point of no return.

Advantages Of Monetary Preparation

The following are 20 advantages of monetary making arrangements for women:

1. Inner serenity.

2. Better rest.

3. Further developed connections.

4. More certainty.

5. Further developed wellbeing.

6. Independence from obligation.

7. Expanded reserve funds.

8. More ready for crises.

9. More cash for retirement.

10. More cash for movement.

11. Better monetary propensities.

12. More monetary security.

13. Expanded riches.

14. Capacity to offer in return.

15. Capacity to seek after interests.

16. Capacity to accomplish objectives.

17. Capacity to make an inheritance.

18. Capacity to leave a positive effect.

19. Expanded joy.

20. Expanded life fulfilment.

I trust these advantages show you why monetary arranging is so significant for women. It's not just about cash - it's about for what seems like forever!

Justifications for Why Women Ought to Have Monetary Preparation

The following are 20 justifications for why women ought to have monetary preparation:

1. To guarantee monetary security.

2. To accomplish monetary objectives.

3. To get ready for life's startling occasions.

4. To turn out to be all the more monetarily proficient.

5. To work on monetary propensities.

6. To accomplish inner serenity.

7. To create financial wellbeing.

8. To feel in charge of your funds.

9. To have the option to reward your local area.

10. To accommodate your family's future.
11. To make a heritage.

12. To leave a positive effect on the world.
13. To acquire autonomy.

14. To lessen pressure.

15. To work on your wellbeing.

16. To have all the more leisure time.

17. To feel more sure.

18. To partake in your life more.

19. To venture to the far corners of the planet.

20. To make your fantasies a reality.

These are only a couple of motivations behind why women ought to have monetary preparation. The advantages are really unending!

Processes On How Women Can Make Monetary Preparation

The following are 20 cycles on how women can make monetary preparation:

1. Put forth clear monetary objectives.

2. Grasp what is going on.

3. Break down your ways of managing money.

4. Distinguish regions to reduce expenses.

5. Track down ways of expanding your pay.

6. Make a spending plan.

7. Keep tabs on your development.

8. Survey your arrangement consistently.

9. Contribute shrewdly.

10. Get proficient assistance if necessary.

11. Make an arrangement for significant life altering situations.

12. Safeguard your resources.

13. Plan for retirement.

14. Lay out a backup stash.

15. Take care of obligations.

16. Construct credit.

17. Set up programmed reserve funds.

18. Expand your ventures.

19. Make a will and a home arrangement.

20. Remain roused and committed.

That is the cycle basically.

Keep in mind, the key is to take little, predictable advances and continue to go in any event, when it gets extreme. You can make it happen!

Chapter Ten

Deep rooted Learning and the Significance of Flexibility

In the present quickly impacting world, it's a higher priority than at any other time to embrace long lasting learning. This implies being available to novel thoughts and better approaches for getting things done, and being adequately adaptable to adjust to change. It tends to be difficult to make changes, particularly when you're OK with the status quo. Yet, it's essential that change is inescapable and it can frequently prompt positive results.

Being available to learn and adjusting has many

advantages.

One advantage is that it can assist you with remaining applicable in your field.

As innovation and businesses develop, the abilities and information that were once applicable may never again be.

By staying aware of the most recent turns of events, you can ensure your abilities stay pertinent and sought after. Another advantage is that it can make you more useful. Groundbreaking thoughts and better approaches for doing things can frequently prompt more proficient and powerful approaches to working. This can save you time and assist you with accomplishing more quickly than expected. Long lasting learning can likewise make you more imaginative and inventive.

At the point when you're continually learning and adjusting, you're continually thinking of novel thoughts and arrangements. This can prompt leap forwards in your work and in your life. It can likewise make you stronger, as you'll be better outfitted to manage unforeseen difficulties and changes.

At long last, deep rooted learning can further develop your general prosperity. Learning new things and extending your viewpoints can be fun and satisfying, and it can likewise support your certainty and confidence. It can likewise prompt better mental and actual wellbeing.

To capitalise on long lasting learning, having the right mindset is significant. You ought to be available to novel thoughts, regardless of whether they challenge your current convictions. You ought to likewise examine and attempt new things, regardless of whether they're outside your usual range of familiarity.

It's additionally critical to be patient and to give yourself an opportunity to learn and develop. You won't dominate everything short-term, and that is not a problem. Be thoughtful to yourself and recollect that everybody learns at their own speed.

At long last, track down ways of integrating learning into your everyday existence.

There are numerous ways of doing this, including:

- Understanding books and articles on various themes.

- Paying attention to webcasts or book recordings.

- Taking web-based courses or going to face to face classes.

- Taking part in meetups or proficient advancement gatherings.

- Interfacing with individuals who have various encounters and points of view.

- Learning another dialect.

- Chipping in locally.

- Attempting new things and testing yourself.

As you learn and develop, it's critical to require investment to ponder your advancement. Ask yourself inquiries like:

- What have I realised as of late?

- How has my reasoning changed?

- What new open doors have I found?

- What difficulties have I survived?

- How am I doing regarding my objectives?

Reflection can assist you with praising your headway, gain from your slip-ups, and make course rectifications when fundamental. It can likewise assist you with remaining propelled and roused to continue learning and developing.

Something last to remember is the significance of equilibrium. While long lasting learning is significant, setting aside a few minutes for different things in your life is likewise significant.

Remember to deal with your physical and psychological well-being, and set aside a few minutes for individuals and things that make a difference to you. By finding the right equilibrium, you can make long lasting learning an economical and compensating part of your life.

At last, recall that deep rooted learning is a deep rooted venture. There's no need to focus on being great or dominating everything. It's tied in with being interested and investigating your general surroundings. It's tied in with tracking down delight during the time spent learning and developing.

Thus, embrace the excursion and take it all in. Be available to new encounters, carve out opportunity to reflect, and track down an equilibrium that works for you. Keep in mind, there's something else to learn!

Justifications for Why Women Ought to Open To Learn

1. To grow your points of view.

2. To acquire new viewpoints.

3. To find new interests and interests.

4. To work on your abilities and capacities.

5. To expand your attractiveness.

6. To remain significant in your field.

7. To be a long lasting student.

8. To remain intellectually sharp.

9. To further develop your critical thinking abilities.

10. To build your self-assurance.
11. To turn out to be more versatile.

12. To stay receptive.

13. To develop by and by and expertly.

14. To track down satisfaction and fulfilment.

15. To acquire a more profound comprehension of the world.

16. To more readily speak with others.

17. To be more open to new encounters.

18. To acquire a more noteworthy appreciation for various societies and thoughts.

19. To turn out to be more sympathetic and comprehend others.

20. To have a beneficial outcome on the planet.
Being available to learn is a vital piece of individual and expert development. It can assist you with turning into an all the more balanced individual and greatly affect your general surroundings.

Benefits Women Will Accomplish By Advancing Consistently

1. Expanded confidence.

2. Better decisive reasoning abilities.

3. Further developed critical thinking skills.

4. More noteworthy imagination.

5. Better memory and mental capability.

6. Further developed relational abilities.

7. More prominent versatility.
8. Expanded efficiency.

9. Diminished feelings of anxiety.

10. Further developed rest quality.

11. More noteworthy inspiration.

12. Upgraded interactive abilities.

13. Expanded energy levels.

14. Worked on emotional wellness.

15. Better connections.

16. More grounded flexibility.

17. Upgraded work fulfilment.

18. Really satisfying life.

19. Long lasting learning keeps you youthful.

20. Deep rooted learning makes you more joyful.

Now that you've found out about the significance of long lasting learning, the following stage is to make a move.

These are a couple of Ways of Starting:

- Put away some time every day for learning.

- Make a rundown of points you're keen on finding out about.

- Discover a few assets to assist you with learning, like books, online courses, or digital broadcasts.

- Evaluate different learning styles to see what turns out best for you.

- Be patient and steady. Learning is a cycle that requires some investment.

You should begin little by defining an objective to peruse for 15 minutes per day, or pay attention to one new digital recording seven days. Or on the other hand, you could begin a task like learning another dialect or investigating a subject that intrigues you. The significant thing is to find something that invigorates you and that you'll be spurred to stay with.

On the off chance that you wind up stalling out or feeling overpowered, make sure to connect for help. There are numerous assets accessible to assist you on your deep rooted learning with travelling.

One incredible spot to begin is by interfacing with other long lasting students. You can track down networks of similar individuals on the web or face to face. These people can offer help, assets, and support as you learn.

Another extraordinary asset is your nearby library. Libraries offer an abundance of information, from books and magazines to online data sets and classes. Furthermore, the best part is that most libraries are allowed to utilise!

Something else to consider is tracking down a tutor. A coach is somebody who can give direction, backing, and guidance as you learn and develop. Coaches can emerge out of varying backgrounds, so feel free to break new ground. It very well may be an educator, a more established companion, a relative, or somebody you respect locally.

At long last, make sure to give yourself elegance. Learning is an interaction, and committing errors is OK.

You could not necessarily feel like you're gaining ground, yet at the same time that is not a problem.

Something else to recall is that long lasting learning doesn't need to be about books and classes. There are numerous alternate ways of learning, like through movement, leisure activities, and individual encounters. Contemplate the things you appreciate doing and how you can involve them as any open doors to learn.

It's likewise vital to require investment to think about your learning. This can assist you with handling the data you've taken in and sort out some way to apply it to your life.

One method for pondering your learning is to keep a diary or log. Record what you're realising, what you're battling with, and any inquiries you have. This can assist you with seeing your improvement and remain spurred.

One more method for reflecting is to impart your figuring out how to other people. Discussing what you're realising can assist you with handling the data and get new viewpoints.

It can likewise assist you make associations and assemble associations with others.

Something else to remember is that deep rooted learning is about something other than obtaining information. It's additionally about fostering your personality, your qualities, and your perspective.

Learning can assist you with improving personally and have a constructive outcome on the world. At last, recall that deep rooted learning doesn't need to be restricted to formal schooling. There are numerous alternate ways of learning, like through self-study, discussions, and travel. Be innovative and investigate a wide range of ways you can learn and develop all through your life.

Now that you know a portion of the rudiments of deep rooted learning, now is the right time to begin. The initial step is to sort out what you need to realise. Make a rundown of your inclinations and interests.

Then, at that point, consider how you can utilise those interests to learn new things.

When you understand what you need to realise, the following stage is to track down assets and potential open doors. Begin by investigating web assets, similar to sites, web journals, and virtual entertainment. Then, at that point, consider nearby assets like libraries, public venues, and meetups.

One more significant part of deep rooted learning is making a timetable. Cut out time every day or week to commit to your learning. It very well may be just 15 minutes or as much as 60 minutes. The significant thing is to be steady and focus on time for learning. How long might you at any point focus on learning every day or week?

Another tip is to track down ways of making learning agreeable. Learning doesn't need to be a task. Search for ways of making it fun and locking in.

You could take a stab at paying attention to book recordings, watching instructive recordings, or playing learning games.

Finally, remember to be patient and give yourself effortlessness. Learning takes time and exertion. You will not turn into a specialist short-term. Permit yourself to commit errors and gain from them. Be caring to yourself and commend your triumphs, regardless of how little.

Deep rooted learning is an excursion, not an objective. Continue investigating and developing, and make sure to partake all the while. Is it true that you are prepared to get everything rolling?

CONCLUSION

The conclusion of **The Lady's Code**: Opening the Monetary Power of Ladies" is that it is workable for ladies to accomplish monetary autonomy and security. By following the tips and counsel in this book, ladies can pursue informed monetary choices, create financial wellbeing, and make a daily existence they love. It's never past time to begin your excursion towards monetary strengthening, so begin perusing "The Woman's Code" today and assume command over your future!

One final direct I'd like toward make about "The Woman's Code" is that it's not just about cash. While the monetary counsel in this book is significant, it's additionally about more than that.

It's tied in with tracking down bliss and satisfaction throughout everyday life, and about taking advantage of the valuable open doors that come your direction. Thus, while the monetary exhortation is significant, remember about different examples you can gain from this book. All things considered, cash isn't all that matters - it's only one piece of the riddle.

To make things one stride further, that's what I'd say **"The Lady's Code"** is likewise about self-assurance. Monetary autonomy and security are significant; however they're by all accounts not the only things that matter.

By heeding the guidance in this book, you'll likewise figure out how to have faith in yourself and your capacities. You'll figure out how to be versatile, how to continue on, and how to transform your fantasies into the real world. Monetary freedom is only one part of a satisfying life, and **"The Lady's Code"** can assist you with tracking down the rest.